sky high

sky high

IRRESISTIBLE TRIPLE-LAYER CAKES

by Alisa Huntsman and Peter Wynne

photographs by Tina Rupp

CHRONICLE BOOKS

SAN FRANCISCO

DEDICATION

In memory of Gramps and Don, our two favorite cake eaters.

A King Hill Productions Book

Library of Congress Cataloging-in-Publication Data available.

ISBN-10: 0-8118-5448-5
ISBN-13: 978-0-8118-5448-1

Manufactured in Hong Kong

Designed by Chen Design Associates, San Francisco
Food styling by Alison Attenborough
Styling Assistants: Chris Lanier and Lilian Kang
Prop styling by Deborah Williams

Distributed in Canada by Raincoast Books
9050 Shaughnessy Street
Vancouver, British Columbia V6P 6E5

10 9 8 7 6 5 4 3 2 1

Chronicle Books LLC
680 Second Street
San Francisco, California 94107

www.chroniclebooks.com

acknowledgments

I would like to acknowledge all of the women in the culinary field, both past and present, who blazed the trail that the rest of us follow. There are too many to name, and each one deserves a sincere thank-you for making it possible for women like me to succeed in our chosen profession.

Thank you to everyone who willingly sampled cakes: My neighbors, Don and Elna Nichols, who accepted each one I offered and were appreciative of them all. My coworkers at the Loveless Cafe, who gave me the chance to work on this project and sampled along the way. And a special thanks to Tony Marchesi for the lesson on making sugared pecans: Your input was invaluable.

My sincerest appreciation goes to everyone at Chronicle Books, especially to Bill LeBlond, who made *Sky High* possible, and to Amy Treadwell, for shepherding this project through every stage.

Thanks to our excellent agent, Jane Dystel. And deepest gratitude to Susan Wyler, whose guidance and support led me through my first book from start to finish.

Last but not least, thanks go to my family: My mother, Carol, who let me walk before I could crawl. My father, Joe Truglio, for believing in me. My mother-in-law, Linda Rubio, for listening to me along this journey. Many thanks to my Aunt Sharon for sharing her guest room and so much more. To Peter for asking me to join him in this project.

And finally, to my husband, Darry, and my daughters, Alix and Devon, who never seemed to tire of eating cake. I couldn't have done this without your support. I love you!

ALISA HUNTSMAN
Nashville, Tennessee

Over the years, a writer realizes that behind every project is a list of contributors about as long as the article or book that bears his byline. Included are family members and friends, teachers and mentors, bosses and colleagues, admirers and critics. In their different ways, all contribute to a project like this, and all are here acknowledged.

PETER WYNNE
Starrucca, Pennsylvania

table of contents

introduction

It can be argued that baking is an art. Certainly, for many it provides an immense pleasure. This book is dedicated to those who love to spend their days—or at least a couple of hours—in a kitchen, measuring, mixing, baking, filling, frosting, and, most of all, delighting in that astonishing transformation that takes place when ordinary ingredients like sugar, flour, butter, and eggs are magically transformed into a glorious dessert. Baking may be more exacting than ordinary cooking, but in some ways it's more alchemical.

Cakes, especially, amuse us with their brilliant rise from batter to rich but light confections, with a delicate and delicious perfect crumb. And if a simple layer cake is one of the loveliest, most enticing desserts to set before a loved one or guest, how much more entertaining the drama of one that is three stories high.

Here is a collection of original triple-layer cakes dedicated to the proposition not so much that bigger is better as that you cannot have too much of a good thing. It also celebrates the drama and delight that a fabulous dessert triggers when presented at a dinner or party. And if an ordinary lushly frosted layer cake causes heads to turn, imagine the reaction to one of these gorgeous sky-high creations.

There's just something so indulgent about three layers of moist, tender cake, given extra height by the silky, sweet frosting that both fills each layer and artfully crowns the top. Keep in mind that the third layer leaves room not only for *more* frosting, but also often for an extra flavor or filling.

More than any other baked dessert, a layer cake evokes warm memories in almost everyone. Perhaps that's because so many of us grew up with a slice of rich chocolate cake accompanied by a glass of milk as a sweet reward. Or because it reminds us of those days when bakeries all across the country proudly displayed enticingly iced layer cakes, tempting both the youngest and the oldest customers alike. A gorgeous home-baked cake is a powerful reminder of childhood parties, weddings, anniversaries, and other family celebrations. More than any other confection you can name, people associate layer cakes with family, friends, and, yes, with love. For what birthday is ever complete without a cake?

Americans prefer their layer cakes tall. The introduction of baking soda in the 1840s, followed by baking powder soon after, had a huge impact on the height of cakes. While Europe is the epicenter for the low, sleek torte, these wondrous leavening agents inspired bakers on American shores to create cakes that rose higher and higher.

If the high, light layer cake is a distinctly American form of dessert, the traditions that surround it and the flavors that inform it come from all over the world. That's why a collection like this is so much fun. If you enjoy baking as a hobby, you'll find many of these recipes both interesting and satisfying to make.

Creating one of these dazzling skyscrapers of the cake world offers entertainment for the ardent, experienced baker and an accessible challenge to the average home cook. Fully dressed—that is, frosted, filled, and decorated—a triple-layer cake is the perfect showpiece to mark a special event. It's not a dessert you can overlook. The mere sight of one guarantees a standing ovation at the end of the meal.

These statuesque confections possess extra height and triple the flavor of ordinary layer cakes. And they are dramatic. There is no way to present either the entire cake or a mile-high slice without eliciting wide grins and a chorus of applause. These are great party cakes that cannot go unnoticed.

Keep in mind, a triple-layer cake is not just a pumped-up version of a double-layer cake. You can't simply up the amount of ingredients and divide the batter among three pans. Such a dessert is far more than three layers of cake. There is the important issue of balance—that is, the relation of height to diameter and cake to filling, frosting, and glaze. Depending upon the recipe and the occasion for which it is destined, and the number of people it is intended to serve, a layer cake might be as small as six inches or as large as ten inches or more in diameter. The height of each layer must be calculated accordingly, or the proportions will be off, and the cake will look ungainly when cut.

Three layers also means much more in the way of creative fillings. Many of these stunning cakes double the pleasure not only with classic additions such as nuts and spices, fruit preserves, marzipan, buttercream, and chocolate, but with contemporary flavors like chai, cappuccino, lime, mango, and ginger. The combinations can be endless and limited only by the imagination of the baker.

irresistible triple-layer cakes

Sky High features both new flavor combinations and updated versions of popular classics. Scotch Whisky Cake (page 145), Marbled Lemon-Blueberry Butter Cake (page 109), Santa Fe Blue Cornmeal Cake with Caramel Cream (page 169), and Dulce de Leche Cake (page 154) will surely take their places next to such established favorites as our versions of Mile-High Devil's Food Cake (page 53), Triple-Decker Boston Cream Pie (page 94), Neapolitan Rum Cake (page 161), and Sky-High Strawberry Shortcake (page 89).

Another advantage of triple-layer cakes is their generous size—perfect for entertaining, especially for holidays and special events. Halloween Sweet Potato Cake (page 178) offers a delightful coda to a casual party. Our gorgeous Strawberry Surprise-Package Cake (page 205), wrapped neatly in fondant, complete with ribbon and bow, is a present in itself, destined to be the star of any stylish table. We've got the ideal child's Ice Cream Birthday Cake (page 183) and a romantically indulgent flourless Chocolate Valentine Sweetheart Cake for your beloved (page 175). And then there are the wedding cakes, so beautiful they may inspire you to tie the knot: Chocolate-Raspberry (page 187), for those who must have chocolate at every important event; Lavender-Rose (page 192), as sophisticated and gorgeous as any cake you've seen, designed as the grand centerpiece for a wedding celebration; and Tiramisu (page 201), a crowd-pleaser extraordinaire.

Some cakes are simply frosted, some contain a separate filling and frosting, and some go all the way with a filling, a frosting, and a glaze—not to mention ornamental decorations. Each cake in this book, with accompanying frosting, fillings, glazes, and decorations, has been individually designed to fit the flavor with the form. Aside from one or two challenging garnishes for the special-occasion cakes, simple piping is the most complicated technique required here. In addition to clear instructions and, we hope, enticing text, we've included separate sections on ingredients, equipment, and technique—all the necessary basics to help you produce the most glorious-looking and best-tasting cakes you'll ever make.

It goes without saying that executing one of these beauties is surely more satisfying than making a cake from a box, and far less expensive than your local supermarket's bakery-case offerings. And the look of bliss on the faces of friends and loved ones as they tuck in to a slice of any of these magnificent cakes will be ample reward. So why settle for two layers when you can have three—sky-high and heavenly tasting!

For home bakers, a layer cake is the ultimate indulgence, the first choice for bake sales and potlucks. And it is for those same bakers and dessert lovers everywhere—especially those who wish birthdays came more than once a year—that this collection of originally flavored, accessible, and simply but beautifully decorated three-layer cakes is dedicated.

baking basics

cake varieties

Following a recipe for a triple-layer cake is a bit like using a set of blueprints to build a house: If you have a clear vision of the structure, it's much easier to follow the plans, and if you know what kind of cake you're baking, the recipe's individual steps make more sense. Of course, you're always aiming to bake a light, tender cake that's full of flavor, but it's easier to get the results you want when you're familiar with basic cake categories.

butter cakes

Most of the cakes in this book are *butter cakes*, meaning the first step of the recipe involves creaming butter and sugar together. Then the additional ingredients (usually eggs and flour) are incorporated. The final addition to a butter cake is its leavening agent—either baking powder or baking soda or a combination of the two. Layer cakes are usually butter cakes, especially if they're baked at home from scratch. As a rule, butter cakes have a fine, tender crumb, moist and delectable. It's the paradigm most of us think of when we hear the word *cake*.

foam cakes

Foam cakes include genoise, sponge, and angel food cakes. The rising action of foam cakes derives mainly from the whipped eggs included in their batters, rather than from leavenings like baking powder or baking soda. Foam cakes have a higher ratio of eggs to flour than butter cakes do, and a spongier texture.

chiffon cakes

Chiffon cakes are a kind of hybrid of a butter cake and a foam cake (and are often considered foam cakes). They contain both whipped eggs and leavening, and they generally rely on oil rather than butter. The texture of a chiffon cake is a kind of cross between the two types of cake as well: A chiffon cake has the moistness of a butter cake but the airiness of a foam cake.

baking techniques

As a general rule, whether baking from this book or another one, you should read the recipe through from start to finish. Then assemble all the ingredients and tools and set out your measured ingredients in their final form. Take any cold ingredients—butter, eggs, milk—out of the refrigerator at least 30 minutes before you start, so they have time to warm to room temperature, unless the recipe specifies that they should be cold.

measuring ingredients

Baking is a great creative outlet, but unlike regular cooking, baking requires that measurements be exact, and the recipes are formulas that need to be followed closely. A cake with only a few extra tablespoons of sugar inadvertently added may sink in the center rather than rising properly.

All the recipes in this book use the "scoop and sweep method" for measuring dry ingredients. To do this, scoop up enough of your dry ingredient from its container to pour into the measuring cup so that it overflows slightly. Then sweep the excess back into the canister by running the blade of a straight-edged spatula or the flat edge of a table knife across the measuring cup's rim. Do the same with measuring spoons for smaller amounts, dipping them directly in the containers.

Measure liquid ingredients in transparent glass or plastic measuring cups (the kind with a handle and a spout) with amounts marked on the sides. Pour the liquid into the measuring cup, place the cup on a level surface, and bend down so that your eye is level with the cup's markings to ensure that the level of the liquid is even with the line. It's best to use the smallest cup possible for the amount you want. The more empty space in the measuring cup, the greater the chance of error. For example, if you try to measure $1/4$ cup water in a 2-cup glass measuring cup and you miss the mark by $1/8$ inch, the amount of liquid will be off by about 1 tablespoon, or 25 percent—a large amount in cake-baking terms.

melting chocolate

The best way to melt chocolate evenly is by using a double boiler. (Some people have good results with microwave ovens, but power can vary widely from model to model, hot spots are common, and it's easy to scorch the chocolate in just a few extra seconds.) A double boiler is simply a two-story pan with simmering water in the bottom that gently heats the top pan. A metal bowl set over a larger pan with water serves exactly the same purpose. With either scenario, it's essential that the bowl or pan with the chocolate be set over—not touching—the water below. Fine chocolate is a delicate ingredient and can scorch easily.

Also, never allow the water underneath to boil; even a stray drop jumping up and mixing with the chocolate will cause it to seize—that is, tighten and dry up. Stir the chocolate occasionally while it is melting and keep a close eye on it. Remove from the heat when there are still a few small lumps, and let stand a minute or two longer; then stir until smooth. Chocolate left over heat too long may turn grainy.

preparing pans

Greasing instructions vary from recipe to recipe. For all butter cakes, plain metal baking pans must be *greased* or *buttered,* which means the interior of each pan should be coated evenly with soft unsalted butter. For these cakes, the bottom of each pan is lined with a round of parchment or waxed paper, which is also buttered. In the past, flouring pans was often called for in addition to greasing, but flouring a buttered pan can result in a crumbly crust that makes frosting difficult, so with only a few exceptions, these recipes don't call for flouring the pans.

Conversely, baking pans for foam cakes—sponge, genoise, and angel food—and chiffon cakes are left ungreased. These cakes actually need to stick to the sides of their pans in order to rise properly. To make it easier to turn out these layers, the bottoms of the pans are lined with parchment or waxed paper. When in doubt, simply follow the instructions for each cake.

If using silicone pans or nonstick metal pans, follow the manufacturer's instructions, which usually involve misting the interior of the pan with a vegetable-oil cooking spray for butter cakes and leaving it ungreased for foam cakes. (If nonstick pans are dark in color, the manufacturer may recommend reducing the oven temperature by 25 degrees F.)

beating batter

Unless specified otherwise in the recipe, all batters beaten with a standing electric mixer should be mixed with the paddle attachment. The whip attachment is called for occasionally to beat egg whites and cream.

When mixing cake batter, don't be tempted to raise the speed above medium, unless instructed to do so. Overbeating causes a dry, dense crumb and a tough cake. The only exception is if you are using a handheld mixer, which might need a little more power. When you're beating a batter, you're always looking for a happy medium—a batter that has been beaten long enough so that it's aerated with lots of the small bubbles that make it rise, but not so long and hard that the flour's gluten is activated.

Most butter cake recipes in this book use the *two-stage method.* That means the shortening (usually butter), all the dry ingredients, and some or all of the liquid go into the mixing bowl at the start and are beaten until smooth. That's the first stage. In the second, once the mixture has been beaten smooth, eggs and any remaining liquid go into the bowl, and the beating continues to aerate the batter. The two-stage method produces a more finely textured cake and is more dependable than the traditional *creaming method,* which is more familiar to home bakers.

In a few instances, the creaming method is preferable. Here the batter is aerated first by beating softened butter with an electric mixer at low speed until it looks creamy, then by beating in sugar and gradually increasing the mixer's speed until the mixture is light and fluffy. Sometimes the mixture begins to look curdled rather than creamy, but all is not lost. Refrigerate the bowl for 5 to 10 minutes; then beat the mixture again until it looks light and creamy.

For either the two-stage or creaming method, the butter should be at room temperature, 68 to 70 degrees F, so that it is soft enough to trap and hold air, but not so soft that it begins to separate. Depending on the temperature of your kitchen, you should remove butter from the refrigerator 30 to 60 minutes before you will be using it. Professional bakers call the texture of soft butter "plastic," meaning it's not melted or separated but soft enough to shape with your hands.

whipping egg whites

Egg whites are finicky. If there is the tiniest drop of fat or oil on anything they touch, they will refuse to whip to full volume. For this reason, when separating eggs, it's always best to use a small clean bowl to collect an egg white and transfer it to a larger collective bowl before cracking the next egg. That way, if a little yolk drips into the white by mistake, you'll only need to toss one egg white—not a whole bowlful.

Whipped egg whites will separate and collapse over time. Cream of tartar and sugar, gradually beaten in, help stabilize them. The way to maximize the rise from beaten egg whites is not to overbeat them. Whip only until peaks are fairly stiff but droop over at the tip, and the egg whites still appear glossy. If you beat until they are completely stiff and at maximum volume, when the cake is baked there is no room for the hot air to expand; the bubbles will break, the batter will lose its structure, and the finished cake will shrink excessively.

whipping whole eggs

Unlike whipped whites, whole eggs are heated before they're whipped. To do this, put the eggs and sugar in the top half of a double boiler and whisk to combine. Place the pan over barely simmering water and whisk constantly until all the sugar has dissolved and the mixture is lukewarm (100 degrees F), warmer than body temperature. Remove from the heat and, with an electric mixer at medium-high speed, beat the eggs until they're very fluffy and almost stiff. If you lift the beaters, the batter that falls from them will form a raised ribbon that lies on the surface of the batter before slowly dissolving into it. This is called the *ribbon stage*.

whipping cream

There's only one trick to whipping cream: Chill your equipment. Put the bowl (preferably metal) and beaters in the refrigerator or freezer for at least 15 minutes. Keep the cream refrigerated until the last minute. Begin on a slow speed and increase gradually as the cream thickens. Like egg whites, cream is whipped to *soft peaks,* and occasionally *stiff peaks*. Overbeating will turn it into butter, so err on the side of caution.

folding

To fold in whipped or dry ingredients (dry items are usually sifted over whipped eggs), push a rubber spatula straight down into the mixture on the far side of the bowl, gradually turn the spatula almost 90 degrees as you draw it toward you across the bottom of the bowl, then lift the spatula through the mixture along the near side, lifting it up and over. Repeat this twice, but the second time, bring the spatula through the middle of the mixture. Now turn the bowl 90 degrees and repeat the process. Continue folding and turning the bowl just until no streaks remain.

filling pans

For triple-layer cakes, it's very practical to use an 8-cup measuring cup or a batter bowl to divide the batter among the three pans. Simply scrape the batter from the mixing bowl into the cup, divide the amount by 3, then pour one-third into each pan. If the batter is too thick to pour, ladle it into the pans, dividing as evenly as possible. Any slight differences won't be noticeable once the cake is frosted.

positioning oven racks

The ideal situation for baking triple-layer cakes is to have a single rack, large enough to hold all three baking pans, set in the middle of the oven. The pans don't need to be in a row (meaning they can be staggered), but there should be about 1 inch of space between any two pans and between the pans and the walls and door of the oven. If three pans won't fit on a single rack, use two racks, with the lower one at least 6 inches above the floor of the oven, and the second roughly 4 inches above the first. There should be at least 5 inches between the upper rack and the roof of the oven. Place two pans on the lower rack, toward the back, and the third pan on the upper rack, toward the door. If you can't fit all three layers in and the batter contains double-acting baking powder, see the sidebar on page 22 for a solution.

preheating the oven

Many ovens require a good 15 to 20 minutes, or even more, to reach proper temperature. Always preheat your oven well in advance to avoid putting in a cake at the wrong temperature or having batter sitting around in the pans while you wait for the oven to be ready. Be sure to position the racks as you want them before turning on the oven. In addition, many home ovens are not accurately calibrated and can

run up to 25 degrees hotter than stated, so if you don't own one already, by all means invest in an oven thermometer (see page 35).

checking for doneness

Baking times are often stated in a range rather than an exact number. This is to account for variations that can occur due to everything from the thickness of the pan to the day's humidity to the whims of a particular stove. Once you put the pans in the oven, resist the urge to open and close the door and check on your cake's progress; you'll only cause the oven temperature to waver. (Of course, if your oven has a window, feel free to peek as much as you like without opening the door.) At the minimum suggested baking time (or, no matter what the timer says, 5 minutes after the sweet aroma of baking cake has begun to fill the room—always a sure sign), open the oven and test the cake by inserting a toothpick or cake tester into the center. When a cake is done, a toothpick will come out clean, and the cake's edges will be just beginning to pull away from the sides of the pan.

cooling and unmolding cakes

Transfer cake layers from the oven to wire cooling racks. Let butter cakes stand, right-side up, for about 10 minutes. Chiffon and foam cakes should be allowed to cool completely in their pans.

To turn out any type of layer, run a small metal spatula or a dull knife around the perimeter. Then hold the pan at a 45-degree angle just above the cooling rack, so that it is almost upside down. Gently shake the pan or rap its side. If that doesn't work, give the pan a quarter turn and shake or rap it again. Repeat this process two or three times. If the layer really seems stuck, put the pan back into the oven for a minute or two to soften any sugar sticking to the bottom of the pan. Once they have been turned out of the pans, allow butter cakes to cool completely before proceeding.

preparing to decorate

If the frosting will simply cover the sides and top of the cake, place the cake on a plate or stand lined around the edge with 4 strips of waxed paper, each about 4 inches wide and 12 inches long. Once you place the cake over the paper, no part of the plate should be visible. After frosting, ease the strips from beneath the cake and discard, leaving behind a clean plate.

Whenever you will need to lift a cake, use a cake board. This is a stiff piece of corrugated cardboard (see page 38) that is designed to support the dessert. Inexpensive and available wherever cake baking and decorating equipment is sold, these boards allow you to pick up the cake for transport or to hold it, if necessary, while you decorate it. Remember, a triple-layer cake can weigh as much as 5 pounds!

filling layers

All assembly should be done with the flat side (the bottom) of the cake up so that the layers offer a neat appearance. If for some reason a layer bakes up with a high dome, trim it flat with a long serrated knife before filling, so it doesn't "rock" or create large gaps. Place the first layer flat-side up on your cake stand or serving plate. Sweep away any crumbs with a pastry brush. Place the filling in the center of the layer and begin pushing and spreading the filling toward the edges with a long, narrow metal spatula, preferably one with an off-set or angled blade. Use the edge of the spatula, taking care not to touch the cake with the blade. Smooth the filling with the flat side of the blade.

Here's a good rule of thumb when filling cakes: If the filling and frosting are not the same, leave a $1/4$-inch margin around the edge of each layer. When you're using the same mixture to fill and frost the cake, spread the filling right to the edge.

frosting a cake

When frosting a dark-colored cake with a white or light-colored frosting, you may want to apply a *crumb coat* first, a thin underlayer of frosting that seals in the crumbs. To apply a crumb coat, brush off loose crumbs with a pastry brush. If possible, place the cake on a revolving cake stand (see page 39); it makes decorating much easier. Set aside 1 to $1 1/4$ cups frosting for an 8-inch cake, about $1 1/2$ cups for a 9-inch cake, so that the remainder does not get contaminated with cake crumbs. Use a long offset spatula to spread the frosting thinly over the top and sides of the cake. Spread the frosting with the spatula, smoothing it to cover the cake as thinly as possible. Chill the cake for 30 minutes to 1 hour, or until the crumb coat sets before finishing the frosting.

To apply a finish coat of frosting, with or without a crumb coat underneath, place a generous amount of frosting on top of the cake, then gently spread the frosting until it reaches slightly over the edge. Leave the slight overhang and work down the sides next. Spread the frosting in one direction only, rotating the cake as you work and adding additional frosting as needed. Apply a bit more frosting than you need. Then go back and, with your long spatula, smooth it out on the sides first. As excess frosting collects on the spatula, return it to the bowl. A ridge will form at the top edge.

To smooth the top, hold the spatula at the far edge of the cake, parallel to the top, and swipe it straight toward you to the center of the cake, removing the ridge from the edge first. Rotate the cake and clean off the blade by returning excess frosting to the bowl and wiping the spatula clean between strokes. Finally, smooth the center. For a very finished sleek effect, heat the spatula under hot water and wipe dry; then run over the cake to smooth the frosting to a glossy shine.

decorating your cake

If you want some texture to your frosting, as opposed to a smooth, sleek look, use an icing comb to make interesting ridges, concentric circles, or wavy patterns. A revolving cake stand, or turntable, will give you an even design, which works well for lines and circles; freehand is fun for waves or more creative designs. You can also use the tip of a spoon or a small offset spatula to make swirls in the frosting or draw it up into little peaks.

One of the easiest ways to make a cake attractive is to decorate the top and/or sides with an ingredient that offers a clue to what is in the cake: shredded coconut, chopped nuts, chocolate curls, berries, or slices of fruit, for example. Edible (that is, nontoxic) flowers, like roses, violets, pansies, lavender, and certain orchids, or candied flowers make lovely displays. Check with your local florist, making sure the flowers haven't been treated or sprayed. Or look in a gourmet green-grocer, where many edible blossoms are often sold in the salad section.

piping frosting

When decorating a cake, never fill a pastry bag more than halfway with frosting. With one hand, twist the bag above the frosting and hold it tightly to maintain pressure. Squeeze the bag with the other hand. Always squeeze from behind the frosting; if you squeeze in the middle, it will come out the back of the bag as well as the tip.

A *shell border* is a classic cake decoration used in several of the cakes in this book. To create a shell border, first fit the pastry bag with a $1/4$- to $3/8$-inch star tip and fill the bag halfway with frosting. Hold the bag with the tip pointing straight down at the cake. Squeeze out a small ball of frosting. When you reach the desired size, reduce the pressure on the bag and at the same time, push the tip down and pull it up and away slightly, creating a small tail. Form the next shell on the tail of the first. Repeat as needed to make a border. You may want to try a practice chain on a sheet of waxed paper before decorating a cake. The practice frosting can be reused.

rolling out fondant

Fondant comes in a thick block that must be kneaded until pliable before it can be rolled out. You want to work the fondant just until malleable; if it is overworked, it will soften too much and air bubbles can develop. If rolled thin, it offers a lovely neat, smooth finish to any cake without adding undo sweetness. But if you roll fondant too thin, it will be hard to handle and will tear. Fondant does not patch the way dough does, but you can always pipe over small imperfections.

Roll out fondant, as you would a pie crust, on a smooth work surface, such as marble or Formica. Instead of flour, though, dust the work surface and the fondant lightly with sifted confectioners' sugar; also dust the top of the fondant. This sifting is important to avoid any lumps, because fondant is unforgiving, and these lumps will leave little pit marks when rolled out. If the fondant becomes sticky, knead in a little sifted confectioners' sugar.

chocolate curls and shavings

Professionals make paper-thin chocolate curls by dragging a large chef's knife toward themselves across a thick block of chocolate weighing at least 5 pounds. The weight of the chocolate is needed to give you the surface space to maneuver. Since most home bakers don't have large blocks of chocolate in the house, here are some alternative methods.

Melt some chocolate carefully in a double boiler so it doesn't lose its shine, and spread it thinly on a cookie sheet or the bottom of a cake pan. When the chocolate sets, scrape it off with a plastic paint scraper or spackle knife to make long ribbons of chocolate. Gently shape the ribbons, transfer them to a covered container, and refrigerate to harden; then break up into smaller pieces. This is a good technique for making large chocolate ruffles, as well.

Shaving down the side of a chunk of dark chocolate with a swivel-bladed vegetable peeler offers a simpler method that yields smaller curls.

TROUBLESHOOTING

Following are a few of the problems you may encounter, their possible explanations, and some quick fixes:

○ If your cakes come out with a high dome in the middle, chances are your oven is too hot. Other causes of domed cakes include overbeating batter or failing to spread the batter evenly in the baking pans.

○ If the top of a cake appears golden and set, but a toothpick tester inserted in the center still comes out with liquid batter clinging to it, cover the top of the cake with a loose tent of aluminum foil for the remainder of the baking time, to guard against burning.

○ If one side of a layer is higher than the rest, the pan was too close to the wall of the oven, or your oven is not level.

○ If your cake layers have mounded or uneven tops, use a long serrated knife to level them.

○ If your cakes are heavy and slightly concave, there are several possible reasons. It may be that the oven is not getting up to the right temperature. In foam cakes, overbeating the egg whites or underbeating whole eggs can cause the same symptoms. Too much leavening or sugar can also cause this problem; make sure you measure carefully.

○ If your cakes are tough or have *tunneling*, tiny pockets of air scattered throughout, overbeating is the culprit.

continued

- If a buttercream "breaks" or looks curdled, chances are the butter was too cold. Place the mixing bowl in warm water long enough to melt a small amount of the frosting; then beat the mixture again. Do this briefly so that only a small amount of the buttercream melts; then beat again. If it still is not smooth, repeat the steps until it is, but take care not to melt too much at any one time.

- If you're whipping cream and happen to beat the cream too much, all may not be lost. If you have extra cream on hand, you can gently stir it in, a tablespoon at a time, until you've produced something that's usable. Do not try whipping the cream again.

- If eggs in the shell are still cold when you're supposed to beat them into a batter, put them in a bowl of warm water to bring them to room temperature quickly.

- If you lack the oven space to bake three layers at once and if your batter is made with a double-acting powder that contains sodium aluminum sulphate, you can refrigerate one of the baking pans while you bake the other layers. This type of baking powder does most of its work as the batter heats up in the oven. When you bake the third layer, you may have to add 1 to 2 minutes to the baking time.

With either method, temperature is key to success. If the chocolate is too warm, the ribbon will smear. If it's too hard, it will come up in shards, which are usable but don't look as pretty.

cutting a cake

To avoid tearing the crumb, always cut cake with a sharp serrated knife. Because these three-layered beauties are so large, you'll need a long blade. Have a tall glass of warm water at hand, along with a clean towel; dip and wipe the blade between cuts.

ingredients

The first step in making any great cake is to choose the best ingredients. Most desserts are made from just a handful of elements, so the quality of each one becomes all the more important. Texture, appearance, and flavor depend on making the right choices. Following are some facts about the components that go into our triple-layer cakes.

There are myriad ingredients in the baker's kitchen. Here you'll find information about the ones included in the recipes in this book.

chocolate

The art and science of chocolate production is a book in itself, so we'll keep our commentary to a minimum. However, you can't make smart choices without knowing a few basics.

Cocoa beans are picked green, then roasted, shelled, and milled into a thick, smooth paste. The result is something called "chocolate liquor," which is composed of cocoa butter and cocoa solids. Generally, the more chocolate liquor—also known as "cocoa" or "cacao"—in a chocolate, the more intense the flavor.

These days, many premium brands market their product by listing the percentage of cacao on the label. In general, the more cacao, the less sugar and the more bitter the chocolate. Formulas for dark chocolate, ranging from bittersweet to semisweet, vary with the brands.

UNSWEETENED

Often called baking chocolate, this is pure chocolate liquor that has been allowed to cool and solidify. Its robust, bitter flavor is mellowed in baking by other ingredients.

SEMISWEET

The lines between bittersweet and semisweet have never been very well defined, and while the two are basically interchangeable, semisweet sometimes has more sugar and cocoa butter than bittersweet. The content of chocolate liquor ranges from 35 to 45 percent, and the fat content averages 27 percent.

BITTERSWEET AND EXTRA-BITTERSWEET

Bittersweet chocolate marked for baking usually contains about 50 percent chocolate liquor. Most premium brands contain 60 to 65 percent, however, which is ideal for the recipes in this book. Extra-bittersweet chocolate is slightly less sweet, but the two are often used interchangeably.

COCOA POWDER

Made from chocolate liquor that has been pressed to squeeze out much of the cocoa butter, unsweetened cocoa powder comes in two basic types: natural and Dutch process. The natural kind is quite acidic. Dutch process, darker and mellower in flavor, has been treated with alkali to neutralize the acid. It's for baking cake layers that are almost black. Natural unsweetened cocoa is occasionally labeled as such, but more often, the package will simply say "cocoa." It produces a cake that is a light reddish brown in color. Always look for either type with a high cocoa butter content, 22 to 24 percent. It will have a richer flavor.

GIANDUJA

Pronounced *john-doo-ya,* this Italian favorite is produced by only a limited number of companies (see page 213). It blends chocolate with finely ground hazelnuts and comes in both bittersweet and milk chocolate versions. Only the bittersweet is used in this book.

WHITE CHOCOLATE

White chocolate contains no chocolate liquor, only cocoa butter. Regulations stipulate that it must contain at least 20 percent cocoa butter, not less than 14 percent milk solids, and no more than 55 percent sugar. Be sure to buy pure white chocolate for baking. The product that contains palm kernel oil or hydrogenated vegetable oil, sometimes called "summer coating," is not suitable for the recipes in this book.

dairy products

Fresh dairy products are crucial for extraordinary cakes. Sweet unsalted butter, full of richness and flavor, forms the backbone of most cake batters. Thick heavy cream and unadulterated whole milk make fine custards, fillings, and frostings.

BUTTER

Silky, luxuriant butter makes a cake batter of unequaled quality. Butter not only enhances flavor, it tenderizes the crumb. All these recipes call for unsalted butter. Since salt is added as a preservative as much as for flavor, unsalted butter is usually fresher, with a sweet nutty taste. Often it is also slightly higher in butterfat—a plus for baking. Grade AAA domestic butter has a butterfat content of about 80 percent, European-style butters, as high as 85 percent. The rest is mostly water.

Choosing the best butter you can find will really make a difference in your cakes. Fresh unsweetened butter has a delicate cream flavor and a pale yellow color. Store in the coldest part of the refrigerator, not in the door. Butter picks up other flavors during storage, so keep it well wrapped and away from foods with strong odors. You can also store it in the freezer, where it will keep perfectly for up to 6 months, tightly wrapped and sealed in a plastic freezer bag.

MILK AND CREAM

Milk is used in some cake batters and is an important ingredient for making custards and fillings. When preparing cakes as special as the ones in this book, use whole milk ($3^1/2$ to 4 percent milk fat), which is richer and gives a better texture than reduced-fat or skim milk.

Two types of cream are called for in this book. Half-and-half, used in some of the cake fillings, contains 10.5 to 18 percent milk fat; light cream, which is virtually the same thing, can be substituted. Heavy cream has at least 36 percent milk fat and is best for whipping. For all practical purposes and for all the recipes in this book, heavy cream and whipping cream are interchangeable.

BUTTERMILK

Originally, this was the liquid remaining after butter was churned. Today it's pasteurized low-fat milk that has been dosed with a bacterial culture for a tangy flavor and a thick texture. Buttermilk is naturally acidic, so some recipes that call for it include baking soda as a neutralizer, instead of or in addition to baking powder. Because these recipes emphasize the nutty tang of the buttermilk, they usually do not.

CREAM CHEESE

It comes in a range of styles, but for all the recipes in this book, make sure to use a full-fat natural cream cheese. Reduced-fat cream cheese (labeled Neufchâtel) will be too soft, and fat-free and whipped products are not acceptable. If you buy packaged cream cheese, read the label and try to choose one with no stabilizers or vegetable gums added as thickeners.

SOUR CREAM

Made from light cream, sour cream has an average of 25 percent milk fat; some premium brands contain closer to 35 percent. Like buttermilk, it has been soured with a bacterial culture that gives a unique taste. Read the label carefully and be sure to choose a brand with no gums, thickeners, or stabilizers.

CONDENSED MILK

Sticky and sweet, sweetened condensed milk is prepared by removing about half the water content from whole milk and adding sugar.

eggs

Eggs vary dramatically in structure, depending upon the temperature to which they are raised and how they are whipped. Cooked, but still soft, they contribute lushness and taste to custards, fillings, and frostings. Beaten and baked in a batter, they act as a leavening agent, causing the cake to rise; provide the skeletal structure of the cake crumb; and add flavor, richness, and color.

The science of eggs is fascinating, but for cake baking it's enough to know why and at what point eggs curdle and whites separate. The yolk makes up about one-third of the egg's weight, and the whites (albumen) the other two-thirds. Raw eggs contain complex molecules of protein that, when heated, convert into strands that stiffen during cooking. If these strands are cooked past a certain point (155 degrees F for yolks and 145 degrees F for whites), they start to shrink and become tough. Above 155 degrees, yolks will curdle. To avoid this, starch, such as flour or cornstarch, which will stabilize the protein, must be added. Whites will become granular when heated too much or when the agitation of beating causes the proteins to become so tough that they pull apart from one another.

In this book, we call for eggs graded "large," which means they weigh about 2 ounces each in the shell. The color of the shell has no bearing on flavor or freshness. Eggs have relatively thin shells that will pick up odors and should, therefore, be kept in the coldest part of the refrigerator, enclosed in their cartons. Fresh and, if possible, organic eggs are always preferred.

USDA-inspected eggs must be stamped with what's called a Julian date, a system that marks January 1 as the first number and December 31 as the 365th. This "pack date" tells the consumer exactly what day the eggs were put into the carton. Eggs should be used within 4 to 5 weeks of this date. Although not required by law, most packers also carry an expiration date that lets both the consumer and grocer know the eggs in the carton should not be sold more than 30 days after this date.

Cake batters are greatly affected by the action of egg yolks, egg whites, and whole eggs. Because eggs act as an emulsifier to keep liquids from separating, they should be at room temperature when they're added to a batter, so they'll blend more easily. Although it's easier to separate eggs without breaking the yolks when they are chilled, at room temperature, whites are looser and able to take in more air for increased volume when whipped. Beaten egg whites should be smooth and glossy, not dull and dry.

flavorings and extracts

Only pure extracts and flavorings should be used in fine baking. Better brands are mellow and not overwhelming. Always choose natural rather than chemically manufactured products. The quality of vanilla and almond extract, in particular, are especially important.

ALMOND EXTRACT

Made from bitter-almond oil, almond extract has a warm, mellow yet intense flavor that should be used sparingly.

CITRUS ZESTS

The thin, colored layer of citrus skin is packed with flavor. Avoid the underlying white pith, as it can be bitter. A medium lemon will yield 2 to 3 teaspoons of grated zest and an orange will yield about 1 tablespoon.

COCONUT EXTRACT

Pure, unadulterated natural coconut extract is hard to find. Unless you live in a large metropolitan area with specialty stores that cater to bakers, you will probably have to use a mail-order or online source. Good coconut extract adds a world of flavor to the Coconut Buttercream frosting for our Piña Colada Cake (page 116).

COFFEE

Some recipes in this book call for freshly brewed coffee and others specify espresso as a flavoring. Just as for drinking, the freshness and quality of the beans will affect the flavor of your dessert. Instant coffee and powdered espresso are not recommended; they tend to have a bitter, dusty flavor.

ROSEWATER

Made from what's left after the distillation of rose petals, this subtle flavoring agent is a surprisingly inexpensive by-product of the perfume business. Rosewater adds a graceful note to Peach Melba Cake with Raspberry Cream (page 79) and our Sky-High Strawberry Shortcake (page 89), as well as to the fabulous Lavender-Rose Wedding Cake (page 192). It's often available in specialty food shops that cater to a Southeast Asian or Middle Eastern clientele.

VANILLA

The arresting aroma of vanilla fills a kitchen with a richness that's hard to describe. It's familiar yet exotic, heady yet subtle. Vanilla, the pod of an orchid plant, is one of the most alluring flavors in the world—second in popularity only to chocolate—and a vital part of making many cakes. There are some distinctions in quality worth noting.

There is a tremendous difference between low-end and high-quality vanilla extract. Vanilla beans, chopped and macerated, form the base for extract. There are no government regulations on the kinds or quality of beans used, so the consumer is left to depend on brands with a good reputation. How the essence of the beans is extracted, under what conditions they are macerated, and how long the liquid extract is aged are the main factors that affect the quality of the product. (Vanilla is one of the world's most labor-intensive agricultural products.)

Where the vanilla beans come from matters, too. Vanilla from Tahiti, which is so distinctive it has been designated a separate species, and the Bourbon blends from Madagascar are considered the best. They are also expensive, but good bakers agree they are worth the price they command. Most major brands use Bourbon Madagascar blends, which will work well for all the recipes in this book. For some of the recipes in the "Vanilla Cakes" chapter, which highlight the flavor with little distraction, you may wish to splurge on Tahitian. It's also worth buying the best whole beans you can find.

flour

The production of flour is a complex process, but essentially, grains of wheat are milled, broken down, sifted, and then further refined. Millers produce many kinds of flour, carefully matching a specific wheat to a particular use. For the baker, the most important characteristic of flour is protein content. Higher protein content means more gluten, an elastic quality that is good for making bread but not for most pastry or cakes. Cake flour has the least protein, or gluten, content and is best for baking tender cakes.

All white flours should be kept in an airtight container, away from heat and moisture. Flour keeps well for about 8 months in a cool storage area and up to a year in a refrigerator or freezer.

ALL-PURPOSE FLOUR

This flour has a medium protein content and is good for sturdier cakes, like genoise or carrot cake. The little bit of gluten it contains helps hold up chopped fruits or nuts added to the batter. Most good cooks prefer unbleached all-purpose flour for better nutrition as well as taste.

CAKE FLOUR

Made from wheat varieties that have the least amount of protein and consequently the lowest gluten of all, cake flour is finely milled and will yield the lightest, most tender crumb. This is the flour used in most of our triple-layer cakes, and all-purpose should not be substituted unless called for.

leavening agents

BAKING POWDER

The rising agent for most cakes, baking powder contains baking soda and one or more acidic substances in a dry form. When mixed with liquid, a reaction occurs that causes carbon dioxide to produce pockets of air that fill the batter and make the finished product light and tender. Most baking powders today are double-acting. First, an initial reaction takes place when liquid is added. A second reaction occurs when the batter is exposed to the heat of the oven. Baking powder will eventually lose its strength, even when stored in a cool, dry spot. To test for effectiveness, add a spoonful to $1/2$ cup of hot water. If the mixture doesn't fizz immediately, it is no longer of any use. As a good rule of thumb, once it has been opened, it's a good idea to replace your baking powder within six to nine months. Some health-conscious bakers prefer to use baking powder that does not contain any aluminum, such as Rumford. It is equally effective.

BAKING SODA

Baking soda is another leavening agent, used either by itself or in conjunction with baking powder in cake batters to buffer an acidic ingredient like buttermilk, chocolate, or citrus. It is activated solely by the liquid and does not have a second rise with heat.

CREAM OF TARTAR

Cream of tartar, or tartaric acid powder, is a by-product of winemaking. It is often whipped up with egg whites to enhance and stabilize their volume. Follow the recipes, but rule of thumb is 1/16 to 1/8 teaspoon cream of tartar per egg white.

nuts

Almonds, hazelnuts, pecans, and walnuts—and peanuts in the form of peanut butter—are used in this book in batter, frosting, and as decoration. Most nuts have a high fat content and consequently are quite perishable in the sense that they turn rancid faster than you'd expect. There is nothing more unappealing than the taste of rancid nuts. To avoid it, buy fresh nuts either in a closed container or in bulk from a source that has high turnover. Store them in a tightly sealed container in the refrigerator or freezer.

Toasting brings out the flavor of nuts. Spread shelled nuts out on a jelly-roll pan and place in an oven preheated to 325 or 350 degrees F.

Roast for 7 to 12 minutes, depending on the type of nut, stirring or shaking the pan from time to time. They're done when the nuts are fragrant and just starting to turn color. Nuts become bitter when overcooked, so watch them carefully. Let cool completely before using.

oils for baking

Cakes made with bland *vegetable oil* or *nut oil* are spongier and more pliant than those made from butter, which results in a crumblier texture. In most cases the recipes that use oil call for "neutral vegetable oil." This might be canola, safflower oil, soybean oil, or a blend. Avoid olive oil, which will overwhelm more subtle ingredients.

A few recipes call for walnut or hazelnut oil. These are not neutral; in fact, when shopping for them, look for lightly toasted, richly flavored oil and pay the price for the best. One note of caution: Nut oil is highly perishable. Once you open a bottle, be sure to store it in the refrigerator so it doesn't become rancid.

spices

The complexity of sweet spices has intrigued bakers for centuries, and recent trends in the dessert world, which has become increasingly sophisticated, have turned to a wider range of flavors. Spices used in our recipes include cinnamon, ginger, nutmeg, cloves, cardamom, and even saffron. Most are ground; saffron threads and freshly grated whole nutmeg are exceptions.

To ensure that the ground spices you use are as fresh as can be, examine the color and aroma. The color should be rich and bright, not faded. Rub some in the palm of your hand so that friction will release essential oils; they should be pleasantly aromatic, not feeble. If the color, aroma, and taste are gone, it's time to buy a new jar. Whether new or aging, spices stay fresher longer if they're properly stored. Keep them tightly closed in airtight containers, away from heat, moisture, and sunlight.

sugar and other sweeteners

Sugar adds both sweetness and moisture to cakes, because when it melts it becomes liquid. It also gives good color, helps to tenderize the crumb, and acts as a preservative.

Most sugar comes from cane and beets, and, in lesser quantities, from palm trees, maple trees, sorghum, and barley. The refinement of the juices that come from these sources determines whether the end product will be granulated, white, brown, or confectioners' sugar.

GRANULATED SUGAR

This mixture of fine and very fine granules of sucrose is the most common type. It is measured with the same scoop and sweep technique as flour.

SUPERFINE SUGAR

Here the sucrose is ground into extra-fine granules that dissolve quickly, even in cold liquids.

BROWN SUGAR

Varying amounts of molasses are added to granulated sugar to produce light or dark brown sugars. All brown sugars derive their taste and color from the molasses content, and in recipes, they can be used more or less interchangeably, depending on the desired flavor. In these recipes, "brown sugar" always means light brown sugar. It should be measured by packing it firmly into the measuring cup before sweeping off the top.

Brown sugar invariably turns into a rock when it is stored for too long after opening and the moisture evaporates. To soften, put a half-pound of the hardened sugar in a microwave-safe bowl. Cover with wet paper towels, wrap in plastic, and microwave on high for $1^1/_2$ to 2 minutes. Break up with a fork, stir, and use at once. You can get the same effect by leaving the damp paper-towel- and plastic-wrapped bowl overnight at room temperature.

CONFECTIONERS' SUGAR

This is finely pulverized sucrose mixed with a little cornstarch to prevent clumping. The number of X's on the package refers to the fineness of the sugar; most products available to consumers are 10-X. Uncooked frostings are often based on confectioners' sugar, which is also used for decoration. Confectioners' sugar will keep almost indefinitely in an airtight container.

CORN SYRUP

This sweetener is made by treating cornstarch with enzymes and transforming it into sugars. The best-known brand, Karo syrup, came on the market in 1902 and from then until the 1970s, the sugar in corn syrup was mostly glucose, which is not particularly sweet. In the 1970s, a new, sweeter form was developed called "high-fructose corn syrup," and today, most corn syrups are a blend of the two.

Light corn syrup is colorless and translucent, sweet, and flavored with salt and vanilla. *Dark corn syrup* is colored and flavored with refiners' syrup or molasses. All the corn syrup used in our recipes is the light variety.

HONEY

Bees make this thick natural sugar from flower nectar. The color and flavor vary according to the nectars the bees have gathered. For baking, a pleasingly flavored honey that is floral but not overpowering, such as wildflower or clover, is recommended. Honey allows cakes to brown quickly and helps hold in moisture.

MOLASSES

This dark syrup is basically concentrated sugarcane juice with some of the sugar extracted. Be sure to buy "unsulphured molasses," meaning sulphur was not used to process it. Unsulphured is the lightest, least sweet molasses available.

thickeners

CORNSTARCH

In some cakes, cornstarch is used to increase the starch content without increasing the protein; this lightens the crumb even further. Cornstarch is also used to thicken fillings, custards, and citrus curds. To prevent lumping if it is being used to thicken a liquid, the cornstarch should first be dissolved in a small amount of cold liquid.

UNFLAVORED GELATIN

This binding agent creates a firm filling that won't melt at room temperature. One packet contains $1/4$ ounce, about $2 1/2$ teaspoons, enough to thicken 2 cups liquid.

equipment

Whether you love to bake regularly or you're a self-designated cook who's most likely to bake a cake for a special occasion, having a properly equipped kitchen makes everything easier and ensures better results. Remember, with a triple-layer cake, you'll have more of most ingredients, so you may need to upsize your kitchen slightly. Here is a selection of equipment you might like to consider.

mixing bowls, cake pans, and utensils for the cake baker's kitchen

MIXING BOWLS

What's different about mixing bowls for triple-layer cakes is their size. Of course, an assortment of variously sized mixing bowls, usually made of heavy-duty stainless steel or tempered glass, gives you a neat place to put everything. A number of smaller bowls are particularly helpful if you do a formal *mise en place*—that is, measure out each ingredient and have it ready for use beforehand. But for those big batters, you'll want to have one or two 6- to 8-quart bowls and a couple of very large bowls (10- to 12-quart capacity). The extra room allows for mixing and folding of these large amounts of batter, as well as whipping up volumes of egg whites or whipped cream. It's always easier to fold properly when you have enough room to maneuver. These extra-large bowls are particularly helpful if you make any of the wedding cakes.

Whipping cream is best done in a stainless steel bowl, which can be chilled first in the refrigerator or freezer. Stainless steel is also helpful for melting chocolate or beating eggs and sugar over a pan of hot water on the stove, creating a *de facto* double boiler. Ceramic bowls are fine for beating batters, but they are heavy and can chip. Hard plastic is lightweight and durable but cannot be exposed to high heat.

If you have a standing mixer, which, of course, comes with its own specially designed bowl, it's usually helpful to own a second if you can manage it. This reduces time spent cleaning up between steps, allowing you to work faster and more efficiently.

GRATERS AND ZESTERS

Handheld graters, usually made of stainless steel, may be flat or box-shaped. The small holes on a box grater are fine for grating citrus or ginger, but there are more specialized tools available that can make much quicker work of these tasks.

The *Microplane* started out as a woodworking tool, a sort of rasp; found its way into the kitchen; and is, today, one of the most popular pieces of equipment for cooks and bakers. Sharp, easy to use, easy to clean, and ergonomically comfortable, the Microplane is excellent for grating both citrus zest and ginger. It's important to keep in mind, though, that a Microplane creates much greater volume than an ordinary grater. So when you're measuring ingredients that you've grated with a Microplane, be sure to double the amount called for. That is, if a recipe calls for 1 teaspoon grated lemon zest and you're using a Microplane, measure out 2 teaspoons.

A nutmeg grater belongs in every baker's kitchen, simply because freshly grated nutmeg has a far superior flavor to commercially ground. It can be a dedicated semi-cylindrical nutmeg grater with a compartment that holds whole nutmegs or a small, flat metal grater with tiny holes. Some boxed graters with handles collect the grated spices at the bottom.

A *ginger grater* is nice to have, too. This flat, one-sided tool with sharp teeth is typically made of porcelain or bamboo. It is designed to grate the ginger while retaining some of the tough fibers.

A *zester* is a blunt handheld tool with small sharp holes at the end of a narrow dull blade. When pulled across the skin of a citrus fruit, it peels away thin strips of the zest, leaving behind the bitter white pith.

KNIVES

Bakers use a *chef's knife* primarily for chopping—chocolate, nuts, dried fruit, and the like—and a heavy knife is best for this purpose. With a little practice, a chef's knife can also be useful for making long, thin decorative curls from a block of chocolate.

Although available in blade lengths ranging from 6 to 12 inches, the 6-inch and 8-inch knives are the easiest for most home bakers to handle. No matter what size, look for a knife with a sturdy blade made of high-carbon stainless steel. The thick joint at the base of the blade, known as the bolster, should be forged from the same steel blank. The part that secures the blade to the knife, called the tang, should extend through the entire length of the handle. The handle itself should be either bonded to the tang or fastened with secure rivets.

You'll also want at least a couple of good sharp *paring knives* with blades 2 to 4 inches long,

for trimming fruit and vegetables. A paring knife with a short, curved blade is handy for cutting fruit slices away from the cores and for peeling round fruit. An ordinary *table knife* with a blunt blade is used to release the sides of sponge cakes from their pans.

For cutting three-layered cakes, a long, sharp *serrated knife* is essential. The toothed blade cuts through the crumb without tearing and is helpful for trimming. A wedge-shaped *cake knife* with one serrated edge is designed specifically for serving slices of cake. Often they are decorative, sometimes made of silver. A cake knife, however, is probably too short for many of these sky-high desserts. With these towering triple-layered confections, it's best to cut with the serrated knife first, and use the cake knife for transferring the slices to the plates.

Prices for knives vary greatly, but price doesn't necessarily determine performance. The heft and balance—how the knife feels in your hand—as well as how well it will hold its edge are the most important considerations.

KITCHEN SCALES

For accuracy, professional bakers measure dry ingredients by weight. However, all the recipes in this book were tested with volume measure, and if you follow the directions and measure dry ingredients properly with the "scoop and sweep" technique, you are guaranteed successful results.

MEASURING CUPS AND SPOONS

Unlike day-to-day cooking, baking is an exact science. A cake recipe is a carefully designed formula that includes exact measurements of dry and wet ingredients and leavening agents, as well as sweeteners and flavorings, to yield a successful result. You cannot improvise and expect your cake to rise properly or have a perfect crumb. Therefore, the tools used are important, and a full set of measuring cups for both dry and liquid measure and spoons are essential for the baker's kitchen.

If you do a lot of baking, two sets of *dry measuring cups* are not an extravagance. Straight-sided heavy-duty stainless steel cups have a nice professional feel to them, but sturdy plastic measuring cups with curved sides are easier for scraping out a sticky ingredient with a rubber spatula. Whichever you choose, it is especially handy to have a set that includes $2/3$ and $3/4$ cup measures along with the usual $1/4$, $1/3$, $1/2$, and 1 cup. Some sets also have a $1/8$ cup measure.

Liquids are measured in *tempered glass* and *heavy clear plastic measuring cups*, usually detailing both cups and ounces, with a handle and pouring lip. It's a good idea to own both 2- and 4-cup sizes so you can use the smallest liquid measure possible. That's because if you measure a small amount of liquid in a large cup, your accuracy will be off by more than if you use a small cup. For dividing batter among the three cake pans, an 8-cup measure is extremely helpful. That way, you are guided by the numbers rather than just by sight.

The dry-volume standard for *measuring spoons* is divided into tablespoons and teaspoons. It's useful to know that 1 cup is equal to 16 tablespoons, $1/4$ cup is equal to 4 tablespoons, 1 tablespoon is equal to 3 teaspoons, and so on. At least one set of good-quality stainless steel measuring spoons should be basic equipment for the home baker, and you won't be sorry to own two.

CAKE PANS

Because, unlike cookie dough, cake batter cannot wait and, in most cases, must go into the oven immediately, you'll need three cake pans for each triple-layer cake. (If your oven is small, we do give a trick for baking two layers and then one [see page 22], but it's still best to own three pans.) Most of the cakes in this book were designed for 8- and 9-inch round pans. A few cakes are 6 inches in diameter. Only the wedding cakes call for larger sizes—10- and 12-inch. A few specialty cakes require square, heart-shaped, or checkerboard pans.

All the recipes in this book were tested in common *heavy-duty aluminum cake pans* that are sold in large supermarkets, shopping clubs, and craft stores that sell cake-decorating equipment. These are relatively inexpensive and conduct heat evenly and efficiently. Older-style cake pans and some less-expensive models are only $1 1/2$ inches high, but if you're buying new pans, go for a full 2 inches. That way, you're sure there will be no spill-over or mushroom-shaped cakes.

Pans coated with a nonstick surface cannot be used for sponge cakes. *Silicone rubber pans*, long used by some professional bakers, are intriguing newcomers to the consumer baking scene. They require no greasing and make it easy to unmold the cake. However, none of these cakes were tested in either of these materials.

SAUCEPANS

These recipes require no special cookware. Quality pans, available in an array of styles and brands, are more easily obtainable than ever. A top-of-the-line, *heavy-duty saucepan* that evenly distributes heat and doesn't react with acidic food, as ordinary aluminum pans do, is a good investment if you don't have one. For making syrups, fruit curds, preserves, and the like, look for heavy-gauge pans made of stainless steel, anodized aluminum, or enameled cast iron.

A *double boiler* is used for delicate tasks like melting chocolate, cooking lemon curd, or thickening custards, which require a slow, less intense, indirect source of heat. It should be made of stainless steel or have an enameled lining, and a capacity of at least 6 cups. For most purposes, a stainless steel bowl set over a larger pan of hot water is a perfectly good, and sometimes better, alternative because of its flexible size.

THERMOMETERS

An *oven thermometer* is a must for successful baking. Even the most inexpensive type of oven thermometer sold in the equipment sections of supermarkets will serve you well. Most standard home ovens are off by at least 25 degrees, and with a cake, this can make a huge difference in your results. If the discrepancy is large and inconsistent, it's a good idea to have a trained technician recalibrate your oven.

A *candy thermometer* is handy for measuring the temperature of syrups. Many recipes in this book call for boiling syrup until it reaches the soft-ball stage, 238 degrees F.

SIFTER

While none of the recipes in this book sift flour to measure—the "scoop and sweep" method is used instead—many recipes call for sifting dry ingredients or confectioners' sugar *after* they have been measured. It's easy because you don't have to be exact, and it's an important step for removing any small lumps, especially in sugar and flour.

This ensures there are no little white specks or unwanted pockets in your finished cake. Sifting also lightens the dry ingredients so they don't deflate the whipped mixtures into which they are folded. There are dedicated sifters with squeeze handles or cranks, which are handy, but a bowl-shaped, one-handled mesh strainer works just as well and allows you to sift with one hand by shaking the strainer slightly.

SPATULAS AND SPOONS

Flat and shovel-shaped curved *rubber* and *silicone spatulas* perform many odd jobs in the baker's kitchen, such as scraping down the sides of mixing bowls and efficiently folding batters. It's a good idea to have several sizes, including a small one for scraping out measuring cups and an extra-large size for these large-quantity batters. Silicone spatulas that are heat- and stain-resistant are excellent for stirring fruit preserves and custards over heat.

A *wide metal spatula* can help lift the edge of a cake, so you can get your hand under the cake board underneath. It's an all-purpose tool in any kitchen. *Long, narrow spatulas* and *offset spatulas* for spreading are especially important for the cake baker's kitchen (see "Decorating Tools," page 38).

Really large *stainless steel spoons,* like the ones that come with a set of kitchen utensils, will be very helpful when you are stirring big bowls of batter. *Wooden spoons* and *spatulas* don't conduct heat, so they're good for cooking, especially if you're using a nonstick pan, and they can be used for stirring batter. If you do use wood, choose a hard one that won't splinter or crack.

WHISKS

A range of *wire metal whisks* in different shapes and sizes comes in handy whether you're a cook or a baker. A very large balloon whisk is needed if you choose to beat your egg whites or cream by hand, something not called for in this book. Smaller whisks are helpful for mixing liquid or dry ingredients and blending anything well. Mixing wet into dry ingredients is impossible with a whisk that's too flexible, difficult with a whisk that's too stiff. The best choice for the baker's kitchen is one right in the middle: somewhat flexible but able to maintain its shape. Whichever one you choose, be sure the wires are stainless steel and tightly mounted into the handle.

appliances for the baker's kitchen

ELECTRIC MIXER

Nothing makes baking cakes easier than an electric mixer. While a few recipes in this book use just a bowl and a whisk or wooden spoon, the volume of batter needed for a triple-layer cake and the aeration desired for many batters, frostings, and whipped cream make an electric mixer most practical.

A standing mixer is one of the most expensive tabletop appliances you can buy, but if you love to bake, it will please you enormously every time you pull it out. When choosing a standing mixer, the most important considerations are power, mechanical design, and speed settings. If you're making the investment, go for the best machine, one with at least 300 watts. Bowl and beater design also affect performance. A 5- to 6-quart bowl will hold 9 to 10 cups flour, or beat up to a dozen egg whites or about 10 eggs and 1$\frac{1}{2}$ cups sugar for a genoise. A mixer this size is large enough to make any of the cakes in this book.

Standing mixers usually come with three typical attachments: a paddle, which is a flat beater; a whisk-like wire beater; and a dough hook. In general, the paddle attachment is used to cream butter and sugar mixtures and mix batters. The whisk attachment is excellent for whipping eggs and heavy cream. All the cake recipes in this book assume use of the paddle attachment unless the whip or other equipment is called for. While the dough hook for kneading yeast doughs comes with most machines, you won't be using it for this book.

Most standing mixers have 10 to 12 speed settings—many more than you'll need for most purposes. A variable slide feature that controls settings between the lowest and highest speeds is available on some models. Speed adjustments of fewer than 6 settings will not give you sufficient control. A machine with a "slow-start" feature will reduce the chances of spraying ingredients out of the bowl on start-up. Keep in mind that these machines are heavy. Unless you have enough space to keep your mixer out on the counter at all times, find a storage place that is easy to reach.

Some standing electric mixers are called "tilt-head models," because the motor head tilts up for removal of beaters or bowl. Others have a lever action to lift or lower the bowl. Whichever you choose, remember that they are all very powerful; you have to be careful not to overbeat when mixing for just one cake—even a triple-layer cake.

HANDHELD MIXER

People who consider themselves cooks rather than bakers and who don't bake often, particularly those with a very small kitchen, may opt for a hand-held mixer. For cakes, this is a perfectly acceptable option, because you don't want to overbeat the batter, or the crumb will be dense and dry and the cake will be tough.

Power, type of beaters, and handle design are the main considerations for choosing a hand-held mixer. You need a minimum of 200 watts; more is better. Beaters with a center post tend to load up with batter and therefore don't mix as well. Wire beaters are better and easier to clean. Look for a handheld mixer that has correct ergonomic features, too. For example, a straight handle forces you to bend your wrist downward. This can become tiring, especially if the unit is heavier than 2 pounds. A handle slanting downward toward the back of the mixer will reduce stress on the wrist and arm. A button that gives an extra burst of power will help with thick batters.

Even if you have a standing mixer, an electric handheld model can still be a valuable addition to your kitchen arsenal. It's good for beating small quantities, and it's portable, so you can beat in a saucepan or double boiler on or off your kitchen range.

Most of the cake batters in this book were tested with a standing mixer and beaten on medium speed. If you are using a handheld mixer, you may need to bump up the power slightly to achieve the same results.

FOOD PROCESSOR

A food processor is handy for baking as a substi-tute for a blender, for pureeing, and for chopping chocolate and nuts. It is, however, a poor choice for whipping cream, beating egg whites, or creaming butter and sugar for cake batters. That's because the cutting action of the metal blades doesn't incorporate enough air.

If you're buying a new food processor, pay particular attention to the capacity of the bowl. A processor with a dry capacity of 11 to 14 cups is help-ful for large-volume work, especially for pureeing large quantities of liquids. Bear in mind that the liq-uid capacity of the bowl is roughly half the stated size. (Liquid will leak from the top rim if the bowl is filled too high.) The 7- or 8-cup bowl is quite all-purpose and best for chopping or grating smaller amounts. For small jobs, such as grating or chop-ping less than a cup, a mini-processor is handy to have, though its power is limited.

Speed settings are not particularly impor-tant in processors, which usually come with just two—"on" and "pulse." The pulse feature—which allows brief bursts that give the user more control—is important, as these machines tend to be power-ful and it's easy to overprocess, particularly when chopping nuts. Some brands come with several speed settings, but this feature is not significant enough to warrant the extra cost.

BLENDER

If you bake a lot, you'll find a blender, with its fast-moving blades, is the best tool for smooth purees. The three most important requirements for a good blender are power, speed settings, and type of con-tainer. Most blenders come with 300 to 500 watts, plenty of power for most bakers. Speed adjustments vary but three (low, medium, and high) and a pulse feature are all you really need. Blenders with glass or stainless steel containers and a capacity of 6 to 8 cups are the best choice. Many professional models, however, come with high-density plastic contain-ers, handy because they won't shatter.

decorating tools

PASTRY BAGS AND TIPS

Learning to use a *pastry bag* greatly enhances your ability to produce a special cake. The three main types of pastry bags are reusable, disposable, and handmade parchment cones.

Flexible, reusable pastry bags made of polyester, nylon, plastic-lined cotton, or plastic-coated canvas are washable and easy to use. Most bakers prefer a large-capacity bag, about 14 inches, which doesn't need to be refilled as often as a smaller version. Disposable bags made of clear plastic are flexible and easy to use. With some care, they can be rinsed out and reused.

In a pinch, cones, large or small, can be fashioned from parchment paper. An opening at one end can be cut to fit a tip of almost any size. For writing or for making very fine details, the cones can be used without a tip. Parchment-paper cones are particularly convenient when several colored icings are needed at the same time.

A *coupler* is a two-part plastic device that fits in the pastry bag and allows you to change decorating tips. The base fits inside the cut end of the bag and the decorating tip is placed over the portion that sticks out of the bag. When you screw the ring on, you lock the decorating tip securely in place.

Pastry tips (sometimes called tubes) come in different designs and sizes, which produce different decorations when frosting is squeezed through them. Shapes like shells, stars, ruffles, basket weave, leaves, and rosettes are a few examples of decorations that can be made with various tips. Pastry tips are made of stainless steel or plastic and often come in sets.

For the decorations specified in this book, you'll need only three tips: $1/4$- and $3/8$-inch plain tips and a $3/8$-inch star tip.

Decorating tips are sometimes designated by number. The only problem is that there are two numbering systems: one for home cooks and one for professionals. The difference is in the overall size of the tip. The complete explanation of the system is lengthy, but, basically, small round tips are in the 1 to 12 range and star tips are in the 13 to 32 range. There are other groupings within these ranges, but they are not as regularly defined.

SPATULAS, KNIVES, COMBS, CAKE BOARDS, AND REVOLVING STANDS

An *offset spatula* or *palette knife* with a stiff metal blade that is bent where it meets the handle is vital for frosting a cake. A good one for frosting large cakes should have a flat blade about 6 to 8 inches long. Smaller ones work well for spreading fillings and for creating certain decorative designs.

Cake boards, made out of heavy corrugated cardboard, make handling, decorating, and transporting cakes much easier. This support is especially important when lifting a triple-layer cake, which is both higher and heavier than an ordinary cake. It allows you to hold the filled and frosted cake in one hand while applying a decoration, like coconut or chopped nuts, to the side. Sometimes plain, sometimes white or covered with foil, these boards come in a wide range of shapes and sizes. They are inexpensive and can be found in cookware and craft shops.

Ridged decorating combs are used to give frosting a textured look. They come in a range of sizes, with fine, medium, and coarse teeth for different effects. If you can find a triangle comb with all three sizes in one, the single tool can serve for all purposes.

An ordinary plastic *spackle knife,* found in hardware stores, is a good tool for making chocolate curls very easily.

Even simple cake decorating is much easier with a *revolving cake stand,* a simple piece of equipment, much like a lazy Susan, that allows you to turn the cake as you work. These turntables range from heavy plastic to metal. There are even electric models, which spin for you. The non-slip pad that comes with most brands is worth having because cakes, especially when set on a cardboard cake round, can easily slide on a stand. A pad is especially important for smaller cakes, like our 6-inch cakes, which don't weigh as much.

PASTRY BRUSHES

Pastry brushes are an indispensable part of a baker's kitchen equipment. They are used extensively in these recipes for brushing syrup over cake layers to moisten and flavor them. They're also handy for brushing stray crumbs from a cake stand or platter.

A dry brush should be available when needed, so it's a good idea to have several on hand. Buy an assortment of sizes for general use. Choose a top-quality brush with a wooden handle and natural bristles. (Inferior-quality brushes will shed easily, leaving behind unwanted bristles.) Wash brushes after each use and store upright or hanging on a nail to keep the bristles straight as they dry.

wedding cake supplies

DOWEL RODS

Like a properly built house, the weight of each tier in a raised-tier cake has to be carried downward to the foundation, and it's *dowel rods* that do the job. Dowel rods can be plastic or wood, but plastic has the advantage in looks and ease of handling: They can be cut to precise length with a sharp serrated knife. Wilton makes plastic dowel rods that measure 3/4 inch in diameter and 12 3/4 inches long and are sold in packages of four rods each.

LEVEL

It's an unusual tool for the kitchen, but a *carpenter's level* is an absolute must for raised-tier wedding cakes. If the tiers are not level, the cake can tumble down. An inexpensive, 9-inch-long, plastic torpedo level, so named for its tapered shape, is probably the most useful. These levels are light and durable; they clean up with soap and water, and can be used to check both levelness and plumb.

PLATEAUS AND STANDS

In wedding cake terminology, the word *stand* usually refers to a cake plate raised on a pedestal, while *plateau* is used for one raised on feet. Plateaus often have a "skirt" extending downward an inch or two below the top, giving the plateau a drum-like appearance. Some bakers have taken to placing each tier of a wedding cake on a separate stand, rather than stacking them in traditional fashion. This gives a floating effect. Such stands can be rented for one-time use.

chocolate cakes

chocolate cola cake with toasted coconut-pecan frosting

While this looks like a classic German chocolate cake and tastes a lot like it, too, this is a contemporary adaptation, a little less sweet, moister, and distinctly Southern with the addition of cola. The original recipe, of course, had nothing to do with Germany. It was developed for the Baker's chocolate company to promote a sweetened dark chocolate they produced, which was named after the chocolate maker who came up with the formula, Samuel German.

1 ½ ounces unsweetened chocolate, coarsely chopped

²/₃ cup buttermilk

3 eggs

1 ³/₄ cups plus 2 tablespoons vegetable oil

1 ½ teaspoons vanilla extract

2 cups sugar

2 ³/₄ cups cake flour

½ cup unsweetened cocoa powder

1 ¼ teaspoons baking soda

¼ teaspoon ground cinnamon

²/₃ cup cherry cola or Dr Pepper

Toasted Coconut-Pecan Frosting (page 45)

MAKES A 9-INCH TRIPLE-LAYER CAKE; SERVES 16 TO 20

1 Preheat the oven to 350 degrees F. Butter three 9-inch round cake pans or coat with vegetable cooking spray. Line the bottom of each with a round of parchment or waxed paper and grease the paper.

2 Combine the chocolate and buttermilk in a double boiler or a metal bowl set over a pan of simmering water. Heat, stirring often, until the chocolate melts, about 7 minutes; do not let the buttermilk come near a boil, or it will curdle. Remove from the heat and whisk until smooth.

3 In a large mixing bowl, whisk the eggs lightly. Beat in the oil and vanilla. Gradually whisk in the sugar until well blended. Stir in the melted chocolate mixture and whisk until smooth and homogenized.

4 Sift together the flour, cocoa powder, baking soda, and cinnamon. Set these dry ingredients aside. In 2 or 3 alternating additions, add the dry ingredients and cola to the chocolate mixture, beating well between additions. Divide the batter among the 3 prepared cake pans.

CONTINUED

5 Bake for approximately 25 minutes, or until a cake tester or wooden toothpick inserted in the center comes out almost clean. Let the layers cool in their pans for 10 minutes. Then turn out onto wire racks to cool completely, at least 1 hour.

6 To assemble the cake, place one layer, flat side up, on a cake plate or stand. Cover the top with about 3/4 cup of the Toasted Coconut-Pecan Frosting, spreading it evenly to the edge. Repeat with the second layer and another 3/4 cup frosting. Finally, spread the remaining frosting over the top of the cake, allowing the excess to drip decoratively down the sides.

7 Refrigerate the cake, uncovered, for at least 1 hour, until the frosting sets. Then cover with a cake dome, large bowl, or plastic wrap until ready to serve. This allows the moisture to even out and prevents the frosting from forming a crust. Chilling also makes the cake easier to cut, something that's best done with a hot, wet serrated knife.

1 cup sweetened flaked coconut

1 cup chopped pecans (about 4 ounces)

2 cans (14 ounces each) sweetened condensed milk

toasted coconut-pecan frosting   MAKES ABOUT 4 CUPS

Note that the method used here for caramelizing the condensed milk in a water bath in the oven is time-consuming. However, it has many advantages over trying to achieve the same results on top of the stove; it requires little attention and prevents scorching.

1 Preheat the oven to 350 degrees F. On a large baking sheet, spread out the coconut and pecans separately. Toast in the oven for 5 to 7 minutes, tossing the coconut once, until the coconut is very lightly browned and the pecans are fragrant. Transfer to a dish and let cool. Leave the oven on.

2 Spoon the condensed milk into a heatproof glass baking dish, cover tightly with foil, and set the dish in a roasting pan or larger baking dish. Fill the pan with enough hot water to reach about halfway up the side of the smaller baking dish. Bake for 2 hours, stirring once or twice, until the milk is a light caramel color. Carefully remove the dish from the water bath and remove the foil with caution; the hot steam can burn.

3 Transfer the caramelized milk to a bowl and whisk until smooth. Stir in the toasted coconut and pecans. Let cool slightly. Cover the frosting with plastic wrap, pressing it directly onto the surface, then refrigerate until cool but not set, 1 to 1 1/2 hours.

triple chocolate fudge cake

Many dark chocolate cakes contain hidden ingredients, and this one's no exception. Mayonnaise is the surprise here. While it sounds retro (and, indeed, did originate with Hellmann's in 1937), there are sound reasons for using mayonnaise rather than oil or butter; it yields an unbelievably moist, tender crumb. That's because the oil in mayonnaise contributes to richness, the eggs to lightness, and the vinegar, which cuts the gluten in flour, to tenderness. In fact, French chefs often add a tiny bit of vinegar or lemon juice to their puff pastry.

While this is a traditional cake, the White Chocolate Mousse filling is quite contemporary. Light and minimally sweetened, it is visually striking when the dark cake is sliced and offers a pleasing contrast to the intense dark chocolate flavor of the cake and frosting.

MAKES A 9-INCH TRIPLE-LAYER CAKE; SERVES 16 TO 20

2 ¼ cups all-purpose flour

1 cup unsweetened cocoa powder

2 ¼ teaspoons baking soda

1 ¼ teaspoons baking powder

1 teaspoon salt

½ teaspoon ground cinnamon

2 ½ ounces unsweetened chocolate, coarsely chopped

1 cup milk

1 ¼ cups hot, strongly brewed coffee

2 eggs

1 cup mayonnaise (see Baker's Note, page 48)

1 ½ teaspoons vanilla extract

2 ¼ cups sugar

White Chocolate Mousse (page 49)

Sour Cream Chocolate Icing (page 49)

1 Preheat the oven to 350 degrees F. Butter the bottoms and sides of three 9-inch round cake pans. Line the bottom of each pan with a round of parchment or waxed paper and butter the paper.

2 Sift together the flour, cocoa powder, baking soda, baking powder, salt, and cinnamon. Set the dry ingredients aside.

3 Put the chocolate in a fairly large heatproof bowl. Bring the milk to a simmer. Pour the hot coffee and milk over the chocolate. Let stand for a minute, then whisk until smooth. Let the mocha liquid cool slightly.

4 In a mixer bowl, beat together the eggs, mayonnaise, and vanilla until well blended. Gradually beat in the sugar. Add the dry ingredients and mocha liquid alternately in 2 or 3 additions, beating until smooth and well blended. Divide the batter among the 3 prepared cake pans.

CONTINUED

5 Bake for 25 to 28 minutes, or until a cake tester or wooden toothpick inserted in the center comes out almost clean. Let the cakes cool in their pans on wire racks for 10 to 15 minutes. Unmold onto the racks; carefully peel off the paper and let cool completely, at least 1 hour. (The layers can be baked a day ahead; wrap well, and refrigerate.)

6 To assemble the cake, place one layer, flat side up, on a cake stand or serving plate. Cover the top evenly with half the White Chocolate Mousse, leaving a $1/4$-inch margin around the edge. Repeat with the second layer and the remaining mousse. Set the third layer on top and pour half the Sour Cream Chocolate Icing over the filled cake. Spread all over the sides and top. Don't worry if some of the cake shows through. This first frosting is to seal in the crumbs, which is why professionals call it a "crumb coat." Refrigerate, uncovered, for at least 30 minutes to allow the icing to set. Cover the rest of the icing and set aside at room temperature.

7 Frost the top and sides of the cake with the remaining icing, which should have the consistency of mayonnaise. If the icing has become too soft, chill briefly; if it is too stiff, microwave on high for just 2 or 3 seconds to soften, then stir to mix well. Use an offset palette knife or the back of a spoon to swirl the frosting decoratively around the cake.

BAKER'S NOTE

For this or any other mayonnaise cake, be sure to use a "real" mayonnaise, and not a low-fat or fat-free product or anything labeled "salad dressing."

4 ounces white chocolate,
coarsely chopped

1 cup heavy cream

1 egg white

1 tablespoon sugar

white chocolate mousse MAKES ABOUT 1 1/2 CUPS

Only a small amount of sugar is used here, since the mousse filling is meant to serve as both a contrast and a balance to the rest of the dark fudgy cake.

1 Melt the white chocolate with 1/4 cup of the cream in a double boiler or in a small metal bowl set over a pan of very hot water. Whisk until smooth. Remove from the heat and let the white chocolate cream cool to room temperature.

2 When it has cooled, beat the remaining 3/4 cup heavy cream until soft peaks form. In a clean bowl, whip the egg white with the sugar until fairly stiff peaks form.

3 Fold the beaten egg white into the white chocolate cream, then fold in the whipped cream just until blended. Err on the side of undermixing.

12 ounces bittersweet or semisweet
chocolate, coarsely chopped

1 stick (4 ounces) unsalted butter

2 tablespoons light corn syrup

1/4 cup half-and-half,
at room temperature

1/2 cup sour cream,
at room temperature

sour cream chocolate icing MAKES ABOUT 2 1/2 CUPS

1 Melt the chocolate with the butter and corn syrup in a double boiler over barely simmering water or in a heavy pan over very low heat. Remove from the heat and whisk until smooth.

2 Whisk in the half-and-half and sour cream. Use while soft.

chocolate-hazelnut nutcracker cake

While this delectable cake, filled and frosted with sweetened whipped cream, is appropriate any time of year, it was designed especially for the Christmas holidays—the "Nutcracker" of the title is a play on the hazelnuts, which are a key ingredient, and the popular ballet associated with the season.

The layers can be baked a day in advance, but the cake is best served the same day it is assembled. After filling and frosting, be sure to allow 6 to 8 hours for the flavors to meld and the cream to set up; otherwise, the dessert will be hard to slice. Leftovers returned to the refrigerator hold their flavor well for 2 or 3 days, but eventually, since the cake contains so little flour, it will soften to a pudding.

1 cup skinned hazelnuts (about 4 ounces)

10 whole graham crackers (5 1/2 ounces), broken into pieces

1 1/4 cups sugar

2 ounces unsweetened chocolate, finely grated (see Baker's Note, page 52)

10 eggs, separated

1/4 cup vegetable oil

1 teaspoon vanilla extract

1/2 cup all-purpose flour

1 1/2 teaspoons pumpkin pie spice

1 teaspoon baking powder

Rum Syrup (page 52)

Crème Chantilly (page 52)

Chocolate curls, for decoration (see page 21)

MAKES A 9-INCH TRIPLE-LAYER CAKE; SERVES 16 TO 20

1 Preheat the oven to 325 degrees F. Butter the bottoms and sides of three 9-inch round cake pans. Line the bottom of each pan with a round of parchment or waxed paper and butter the paper. Dust with flour; tap out any excess.

2 Spread the nuts out on a baking sheet and toast for 10 to 12 minutes, until fragrant and lightly browned. Let cool completely. Increase the oven temperature to 350 degrees F.

3 In a food processor, grind the graham crackers to crumbs. Dump into a bowl and set aside. Without rinsing the processor, add the hazelnuts and 1/4 cup of the sugar to the work bowl and pulse until the nuts are finely ground; do not overprocess to a paste. Add the nuts and grated chocolate to the graham cracker crumbs. Toss together well.

4 In a large bowl with an electric mixer, beat together the egg yolks and 1/2 cup of the sugar until well blended. Add the oil and vanilla and continue beating until a slowly dissolving ribbon forms when the beaters are lifted. Fold in the chocolate-nut-crumb mixture.

CONTINUED

5 Put the egg whites in a large, clean mixer bowl. With an electric mixer on medium-high speed, beat the egg whites until foamy. Gradually add the remaining $1/2$ cup sugar and continue beating on high speed until the whites form stiff peaks. Fold a third of the beaten egg whites into the egg yolk mixture. Using a sieve or sifter, dust the flour, pumpkin pie spice, and baking powder over the batter and fold in. Gently fold in the remainder of the egg whites just until no streaks remain; do not overmix. Divide the batter among the 3 prepared cake pans.

6 Bake the cake layers for 25 to 30 minutes, or until a cake tester or wooden toothpick stuck into the center comes out clean. Let the layers cool in their pans on wire racks for about 10 minutes; then turn out onto racks to cool completely, at least 1 hour.

7 To assemble the cake, place a layer on a cake stand or serving plate, flat side up. Sprinkle with a third of the Rum Syrup and let it soak in for a minute or two. Spread $3/4$ cup Crème Chantilly over the layer, smoothing it right to the edge. Repeat these steps with the second layer. Finally, add the third layer, sprinkle it with syrup, and let it soak in as before. Spread the remaining Crème Chantilly over the top and sides of the cake. Decorate with chocolate curls.

BAKER'S NOTE

To grate chocolate finely without causing it to soften and become messy, refrigerate or freeze the chocolate until thoroughly chilled before grating.

$1/4$ cup sugar

$1/4$ cup water

$1/4$ cup dark rum

rum syrup   MAKES ABOUT $3/4$ CUP

Combine the sugar and water in a small saucepan. Place over medium heat, stirring until the sugar dissolves. Remove from the heat and add the rum. Let cool before using.

2 cups heavy cream

3 tablespoons confectioners' sugar

1 $1/2$ teaspoons vanilla extract

crème chantilly   MAKES ABOUT 4 CUPS

Combine the cream, sugar, and vanilla in a chilled bowl and whip until the cream is stiff but not buttery.

mile-high devil's food cake

You have a choice of two frostings here: a mock Brown Sugar Seven-Minute Frosting and a Brown Sugar Buttercream. The buttercream is, of course, heavenly, but if you don't feel like packing away a pound of butter, you may prefer the lighter frosting. Whichever you choose, the cake will disappear before you turn around.

1 cup unsweetened cocoa powder, *not* Dutch process (see Baker's Note, page 55)

1 1/4 cup hot water

3 cups packed light brown sugar

2 2/3 cups cake flour

1 1/2 teaspoons baking soda

3/4 teaspoon salt

2 sticks plus 2 tablespoons (9 ounces) unsalted butter, at room temperature

3 eggs

1 1/2 teaspoons vanilla extract

3/4 cup cold water

Brown Sugar Seven-Minute Frosting (page 54) (see Baker's Note, page 55) or Brown Sugar Buttercream (page 55) (see Baker's Note, page 55)

MAKES AN 8-INCH TRIPLE-LAYER CAKE; SERVES 12 TO 16

1 Preheat the oven to 325 degrees F. Butter the bottoms and sides of three 8-inch round cake pans. Line the bottom of each pan with a round of parchment or waxed paper and grease the paper.

2 Place the cocoa powder in a medium bowl. Add the hot water and whisk until smooth. Let cool to room temperature.

3 In a large mixer bowl, combine the brown sugar, flour, baking soda, and salt. With the mixer on low, blend to mix. Add the butter and dissolved cocoa and beat briefly to blend. Then raise the speed to medium and beat until light and fluffy, about 2 minutes.

4 In a medium bowl, whisk the eggs with the vanilla and cold water until blended. Add this liquid to the batter in 3 additions, scraping down the sides well and mixing only to incorporate between additions. Divide the batter among the 3 prepared cake pans.

5 Bake for 35 to 40 minutes, or until a cake tester or wooden toothpick inserted into the center comes out almost clean, with just a few crumbs sticking to the pick. Let cool in the pan for 15 minutes. Invert onto wire racks, carefully peel off the paper liners, and let cool completely.

CONTINUED

6 To assemble the cake, choose one of the frosting recipes. Place one cake layer, flat side up, on a cake stand or serving plate. Cover it with about ²/₃ cup of frosting. Repeat with the next layer and top it with the final layer. Frost the top and sides of the cake with the remaining frosting. If you chose the Brown Sugar Seven-Minute Frosting, you can make swirls and peaks by tapping the frosting with a palette knife or the back of a spoon and pulling away quickly. Do this all over the cake, and it will have large breaking waves like a lemon meringue pie. The Brown Sugar Buttercream will not stand up like this; simply frost and swirl gently.

6 egg whites

1 ¹/₂ cups brown sugar

¹/₄ cup light corn syrup

2 tablespoons water

¹/₂ teaspoon cream of tartar

brown sugar seven-minute frosting
MAKES ABOUT 5 CUPS

Brown sugar gives ordinary boiled frosting, which can be cloying, a slightly darker hint of caramel flavor. Do not try to make this recipe on a rainy day. Humidity makes meringue very hard to work with.

1 Put the egg whites into a large mixer bowl. Set them aside at room temperature while you make a syrup.

2 In a small heavy saucepan, combine the brown sugar, corn syrup, and water. Bring to a boil over medium-low heat, stirring to dissolve the sugar. Continue to boil, washing down the sides of the pot with a wet pastry brush, until the syrup reaches the soft-ball stage, 238 degrees F on a candy thermometer. Immediately remove from the heat.

3 Add the cream of tartar to the egg whites in the mixer bowl and beat briefly to blend. With the mixer on medium speed, gradually pour in the syrup in a thin stream, taking care not to hit the beaters. Beat until fairly stiff peaks form but the frosting is spreadable. If the meringue is too stiff, the frosting will be difficult to work with. Use at once.

5 egg whites

1 ¼ cups packed brown sugar

¼ cup water

1 pound (16 ounces) unsalted butter,
at room temperature

BAKER'S NOTES

○ The reason Dutch process cocoa is not
used in this recipe is that a devil's food
cake is traditionally redder than black,
and alkalized cocoa yields a blacker color.

○ Keep in mind that a seven-minute
frosting does not do well in high
humidity. Meringue is extremely hard
to make in summer. Also, it does not
hold up as well as other frostings and
is best eaten the day it is made.

○ Refrigerating a cake frosted with a
meringue is not a good idea. The cake
will firm up, making it harder to cut
while the meringue will remain soft,
so the layers will slide apart.

○ If you choose the buttercream frosting,
the cake can be refrigerated for up to
3 days. Just be sure to let the dessert
return to room temperature before
serving, 1 ½ to 2 hours; otherwise the
frosting will be too heavy.

brown sugar buttercream   MAKES ABOUT 5 CUPS

1 Place the egg whites in a large mixer bowl and set aside.

2 In a heavy medium saucepan, combine the brown
sugar and water. Cook over medium heat, stirring occasionally to dissolve the sugar. Then bring to a boil and
cook without stirring until the syrup reaches the soft-ball
stage, 238 degrees F on a candy thermometer.

3 Begin beating the egg whites with the electric mixer set
on medium-low speed. Gradually pour in the sugar syrup
in a slow, steady stream, taking care not to hit the beaters.
Increase the mixer speed to medium-high and beat until
the meringue cools to body temperature.

4 With the mixer on medium-low, add the butter 1 to
2 tablespoons at a time. When all the butter has been added,
raise the speed to medium and beat until the frosting almost
appears to separate. Continue beating, and it will suddenly
come together, looking like smooth whipped butter.

mocha cake with espresso drizzle

This simple dessert, especially for coffee lovers, requires no beating of egg whites or whipping of cream. It's a quick cake, not even frosted, with a flavor that's on the sophisticated side.

1 cup freshly brewed espresso or double-strength coffee

²/₃ cup unsweetened cocoa powder, preferably Dutch process (see Baker's Note)

4 eggs

²/₃ cup buttermilk

1 ¹/₂ teaspoons vanilla extract

2 ²/₃ cups cake flour

2 ²/₃ cups sugar

³/₄ teaspoon baking powder

¹/₂ teaspoon salt

2 sticks (8 ounces) unsalted butter, at room temperature

Espresso Drizzle (page 58)

MAKES AN 8-INCH TRIPLE-LAYER CAKE; SERVES 12 TO 16

1 Preheat the oven to 350 degrees F. Butter the bottoms and sides of three 8-inch round cake pans or coat with vegetable cooking spray. Line the bottom of each pan with a round of parchment or waxed paper and grease the paper.

2 In a medium bowl, combine the hot espresso and cocoa powder, stirring to dissolve the cocoa. Let this mocha mixture stand until cooled to body temperature. Meanwhile, in another bowl, beat the eggs lightly. Whisk in the buttermilk and vanilla until well mixed.

3 Place the flour, sugar, baking powder, and salt in a large mixing bowl. With the mixer on low, evenly blend the dry ingredients. Add the butter and the mocha mixture, beating until well blended. Raise the mixer speed to medium and beat until light and fluffy, then add the buttermilk-egg mixture in 3 additions, scraping well and blending only to incorporate. Divide the batter among the 3 prepared pans.

4 Bake the cake layers for 35 to 38 minutes, or until a cake tester or wooden toothpick inserted in the center comes out almost clean but still moist. Let cool in the pans for about 10 minutes, then invert onto wire racks. Carefully peel off the paper liners and let the layers cool completely.

CONTINUED

BAKER'S NOTES

o Dutch process cocoa produces a very attractive dark cake here. However, if all you have is regular cocoa, it will taste fine but look redder and lighter in color.

o Because this is such a moist cake, you'll notice the baking time is slightly longer than usual.

5 To assemble the cake, place one layer, flat side up, on a cake stand or serving plate. Pour ½ cup of the Espresso Drizzle onto the center of the layer and spread all the way to the edge, allowing it to drip slightly over the sides. Repeat with the second layer. Set the third layer in place, then pour the remaining drizzle on top and spread to the edges, making sure the glaze drips down the sides, covering all the edges.

12 ounces good-quality white chocolate

3/4 cup sweetened condensed milk

6 tablespoons freshly brewed espresso or double-strength coffee

espresso drizzle   MAKES ABOUT 1½ CUPS

1 Melt the white chocolate in a double boiler or in a medium heatproof bowl over a pan of very hot water.

2 Whisk in the sweetened condensed milk and espresso and continue whisking until smooth. Use while warm.

chocolate cake with almond cream filling, bittersweet frosting, and apricot preserves

When a special someone requests a chocolate birthday cake, this is the perfect choice. Moist, tender chocolate layers are filled with a lush almond-flavored filling and frosted with an intense fudgy ganache. Apricot preserves glaze the top, adding a pleasing counterpoint of tartness as well as a lovely sheen.

6 ounces unsweetened chocolate, coarsely chopped

1 ¼ cups sugar

½ cup strongly brewed coffee

1 ¾ cups all-purpose flour

3 tablespoons unsweetened cocoa powder

1 teaspoon baking soda (see Baker's Note, page 60)

½ teaspoon baking powder

1 stick (4 ounces) unsalted butter

½ cup honey, preferably dark honey, such as chestnut or buckwheat (see Baker's Note, page 60)

3 eggs

2 teaspoons vanilla extract

½ teaspoon almond extract

⅔ cup buttermilk

Almond Cream Filling (page 60)

½ cup apricot preserves

Bittersweet Frosting (page 61)

MAKES AN 8-INCH TRIPLE-LAYER CAKE; SERVES 12 TO 16

1 Preheat the oven to 350 degrees F. Butter the bottoms and sides of three 8-inch round cake pans. Dust with flour; invert and tap out any excess.

2 Combine the chocolate with ½ cup of the sugar and the coffee in a heatproof glass bowl. Microwave on high power for 1 to 2 minutes, until the chocolate is soft when stirred (it won't look melted), then stir to blend well.

3 Sift together the flour, cocoa powder, baking soda, and baking powder. Set these dry ingredients aside.

4 With an electric mixer, cream together the butter and remaining ¾ cup sugar. On medium-high speed, beat in the honey, then the eggs, one at a time, and finally the vanilla and almond extracts. On low speed, add the dry ingredients in 2 or 3 additions, alternating with the buttermilk. Finally, beat in the melted chocolate. Pour a third of the batter into each baking pan. Tap the pans gently on the counter to settle any air bubbles.

5 Bake for 20 to 25 minutes, or until a cake tester or wooden toothpick stuck into the center of each layer comes out clean. The cake should be just pulling away from the sides of the pan and should spring back when touched lightly. Let the cake layers cool in their pans for 10 minutes, then turn out onto wire racks to cool completely, at least 1 hour.

CONTINUED

○ In a slightly unusual twist, this cake calls for more baking soda than baking powder. That's because baking soda is the leavening of choice when dealing with acidic ingredients, and in this recipe, four of the ingredients present varying degrees of acidity: chocolate, coffee, honey, and buttermilk.

○ The batter here is sweetened with both sugar and honey. Besides its rich mellow flavor, honey is highly hygroscopic, which means it retains moisture and, hence, allows the cake to remain fresh longer.

2 whole eggs

1 egg yolk

$^1/_2$ cup sugar

$^1/_4$ cup plus 2 tablespoons all-purpose flour

1 $^1/_2$ cups milk

2 teaspoons almond extract

1 teaspoon vanilla extract

6 To assemble the cake, put one layer on a cake stand or serving dish, flat side up. Cover with half of the chilled Almond Cream Filling, spreading it evenly, leaving a $^1/_4$-inch margin around the edge. Add a second layer, again flat side up, and cover with the remaining Almond Cream in the same fashion. Top with the third layer, flat side up, and spread the apricot preserves over the top of the cake to the very edge.

7 Finally, cover the sides of the cake generously with about three-quarters of the Bittersweet Frosting. Using a small star tip, pipe a rim around the edge of the cake. Pipe out a few small rosettes with any remaining frosting.

almond cream filling   MAKES ABOUT 1 $^1/_2$ CUPS

Since this filling is used cold, it's good to know that you can prepare it up to a day in advance.

1 In a small bowl, beat the whole eggs and egg yolk until well mixed.

2 In a heavy saucepan, combine the sugar and flour. Very gradually whisk in about $^1/_2$ cup of the milk until smooth. Now whisk in the eggs and the remaining milk. Bring to a boil over medium heat, stirring gently and constantly. Reduce the heat slightly and cook for 3 minutes, stirring constantly.

3 Remove from the heat and stir in the almond and vanilla extracts. Let cool slightly. Cover with plastic wrap, pressing it directly onto the surface of the filling to prevent a skin from forming. Refrigerate until thoroughly chilled before using.

8 ounces bittersweet chocolate

3/4 cup heavy cream

3 tablespoons unsalted butter

2 tablespoons Myers's
or another very dark rum

bittersweet frosting   MAKES ABOUT 2 CUPS

1   Coarsely chop the chocolate and put it into a food processor.

2   In a heavy saucepan, scald the cream—little bubbles will form around the edge—but don't let it boil. Finely chop the chocolate in the processor and with the machine on, add the steaming hot cream through the feed tube. Process until the mixture is smooth, then transfer to a stainless steel bowl.

3   Whisk in the butter until melted and blended. Let the frosting cool slightly, then whisk in the rum. Cover and refrigerate until the frosting just begins to thicken; be careful not to let it get too thick. Then whisk the frosting until it is fluffy and smooth. If it gets too thick, you can restore it by putting the bowl in a pan of warm—not hot—water for a few seconds until it softens slightly, then whisk to the proper consistency.

sour cream–chocolate cake with peanut butter frosting and chocolate–peanut butter glaze

This is an easy recipe that doesn't even require an electric mixer. It's a black cake with moist, intensely chocolate flavor, a generous amount of gooey peanut butter frosting, and a peanut butter–chocolate glaze, just for good measure. It is guaranteed to be the star of any party.

2 cups all-purpose flour

2 1/2 cups sugar

3/4 cup unsweetened cocoa powder, preferably Dutch process

2 teaspoons baking soda

1 teaspoon salt

1 cup neutral vegetable oil, such as canola, soybean, or vegetable blend

1 cup sour cream

1 1/2 cups water

2 tablespoons distilled white vinegar

1 teaspoon vanilla extract

2 eggs

Peanut Butter Frosting (page 64)

Chocolate–Peanut Butter Glaze (page 65)

1/2 cup coarsely chopped peanut brittle

MAKES AN 8-INCH TRIPLE-LAYER CAKE; SERVES 12 TO 16

1 Preheat the oven to 350 degrees F. Butter the bottoms and sides of three 8-inch round cake pans. Line the bottom of each pan with a round of parchment or waxed paper and butter the paper.

2 Sift the flour, sugar, cocoa powder, baking soda, and salt into a large bowl. Whisk to combine them well. Add the oil and sour cream and whisk to blend. Gradually beat in the water. Blend in the vinegar and vanilla. Whisk in the eggs and beat until well blended. Scrape down the sides of the bowl and be sure the batter is well mixed. Divide among the 3 prepared cake pans.

3 Bake for 30 to 35 minutes, or until a cake tester or wooden toothpick inserted in the center comes out almost clean. Let cool in the pans for about 20 minutes. Invert onto wire racks, carefully peel off the paper liners, and let cool completely.

4 To frost the cake, place one layer, flat side up, on a cake stand or large serving plate. Spread 2/3 cup of the Peanut Butter Frosting evenly over the top. Repeat with the next layer. Place the last layer on top and frost the top and sides of the cake with the remaining frosting.

CONTINUED

5 To decorate with the Chocolate–Peanut Butter Glaze, put the cake plate on a large baking sheet to catch any drips. Simply pour the glaze over the top of the cake, and using an offset spatula, spread it evenly over the top just to the edges so that it runs down the sides of the cake in long drips. Refrigerate, uncovered, for at least 30 minutes to allow the glaze and frosting to set completely. Remove about 1 hour before serving. Decorate the top with chopped peanut brittle.

10 ounces cream cheese, at room temperature

1 stick (4 ounces) unsalted butter, at room temperature

5 cups confectioners' sugar, sifted

$2/3$ cup smooth peanut butter (see Baker's Note, facing page)

peanut butter frosting   MAKES ABOUT 5 CUPS

1 In a large bowl with an electric mixer, beat the cream cheese and butter until light and fluffy. Gradually add the confectioners' sugar 1 cup at a time, mixing thoroughly after each addition and scraping down the sides of the bowl often. Continue to beat on medium speed until light and fluffy, 3 to 4 minutes.

2 Add the peanut butter and beat until thoroughly blended.

8 ounces semisweet chocolate,
coarsely chopped

3 tablespoons smooth peanut butter
(see Baker's Note)

2 tablespoons light corn syrup

1/2 cup half-and-half

BAKER'S NOTE

This is one of the few places where fresh and natural is not your first choice. Commercial hydrogenated peanut butter works best in this recipe, because the oil does not separate out.

chocolate–peanut butter glaze   MAKES ABOUT 1 1/2 CUPS

1 In the top of a double boiler or in a bowl set over simmering water, combine the chocolate, peanut butter, and corn syrup. Cook, whisking often, until the chocolate is melted and the mixture is smooth.

2 Remove from the heat and whisk in the half-and-half, beating until smooth. Use while still warm.

vanilla cakes

buttermilk sponge cake with cranberry-raspberry preserves and white chocolate frosting

○○○

An easy-to-make jewel-colored filling adds a decorative ruby stripe to this light vanilla cake. By using dried cranberries and frozen raspberries, the recipe can become a year-round favorite. If you omit the frosting, it's even heart-healthful.

2 ¹/₂ cups cake flour

2 cups sugar

1 ¹/₂ teaspoons baking soda

9 egg whites

¹/₄ teaspoon cream of tartar

1 cup plus 2 tablespoons buttermilk

¹/₃ cup vegetable oil

1 ¹/₂ teaspoons vanilla extract

Cranberry-Raspberry Preserves (page 70)

White Chocolate Frosting (page 71)

MAKES A 9-INCH TRIPLE-LAYER CAKE; SERVES 16 TO 20

1 Preheat the oven to 350 degrees F. Line the bottoms of three ungreased 9-inch round cake pans with a round of parchment or waxed paper. Do not grease.

2 Sift together the flour, 1 cup of the sugar, and the baking soda. Set these dry ingredients aside.

3 In a large clean mixer bowl, whip the egg whites with the cream of tartar until frothy with an electric mixer on high speed. Slowly add the remaining 1 cup sugar and continue whipping until soft peaks form.

4 In a large bowl, whisk together the buttermilk, oil, and vanilla until well blended. Spoon one-fourth of the whipped egg whites on top of the buttermilk mixture, then sift a third of the dry ingredients on top. Fold gently until just a few streaks remain. Repeat two more times, then add the remaining egg whites and fold in gently. Divide the batter among the 3 prepared cake pans.

5 Bake for 20 to 22 minutes, until a cake tester or wooden toothpick stuck into the center of each layer comes out clean. Transfer to wire racks and let the cakes cool completely in their pans, at least 1 hour, before turning out. Run a blunt knife around the rim of the pan. Carefully peel off the paper liners.

CONTINUED

6 To assemble the cake, put one layer, flat side up, onto a cake stand or serving plate. Spread half the Cranberry-Raspberry Preserves over the cake, leaving a $1/4$-inch margin around the edges. Top with the second layer; cover with the remaining preserves. Finally, put the third layer in place and frost the sides and top of the cake with the White Chocolate Frosting.

3 cups fresh raspberries or 12 ounces frozen unsweetened raspberries, thawed completely, with juices reserved (3 to 3 $1/2$ cups frozen) (see Baker's Note, facing page)

1 cup dried cranberries

$3/4$ cup sugar

$1/4$ cup orange juice, preferably freshly squeezed

2 teaspoons grated orange zest

1 one-inch piece of vanilla bean

cranberry-raspberry preserves   MAKES ABOUT 2 CUPS

You'll end up with about half a cup more of this filling than is needed for the cake. Marvelous on muffins or toast in the morning.

1 Put all the ingredients except the vanilla bean into a heavy nonreactive saucepan, preferably enameled cast iron. Split the piece of vanilla bean lengthwise without cutting all the way through. With the tip of a small knife, scrape the tiny vanilla seeds into the saucepan. Toss in the bean pod, too.

2 Bring to a boil over medium heat, stirring to dissolve the sugar. Reduce the heat slightly and continue to boil until the preserves visibly thicken, 15 to 20 minutes. To check for thickness, place a spoonful on a glass or china saucer and place in the freezer to cool for a few minutes. If it is ready, it will leave a clear path when you drag a finger through it and will not run. If necessary, boil several minutes longer and then retest.

3 Remove and discard the vanilla bean pod. Let the preserves cool completely, then cover and refrigerate until ready to use. They will keep well for up to 2 weeks.

3 ounces white chocolate,
coarsely chopped

1 cup sugar

$^1/_4$ cup water

3 egg whites

3 sticks (12 ounces) unsalted butter,
at room temperature

white chocolate frosting   MAKES ABOUT 4 CUPS

1   Melt the white chocolate in a microwave oven on low
power for 20 to 30 seconds, until the chocolate is soft and
shiny; it will not look melted until you stir it. Set it aside to
cool. (You don't want the warm chocolate to melt the butter.)

2   In a small heavy saucepan, combine the sugar and water
to make a thick paste. Bring to a boil, stirring to dissolve
the sugar. Continue to cook over medium-low heat without
stirring, washing any sugar crystals down the sides of
the pan with a wet pastry brush, until the syrup reaches the
soft-ball stage, 238 degrees F on a candy thermometer.

3   Put the egg whites into a large mixer bowl, set the mixer
at medium speed, and beat for about 30 seconds. Gradually
pour in the sugar syrup in a thin stream, being careful
not to pour it onto the beaters. Raise the mixer speed to
medium-high and whip until the meringue has cooled to
body temperature, which will take several minutes.

4   Gradually beat in the butter a few tablespoons at a
time, then add the melted white chocolate and beat until
the frosting is smooth and fluffy.

vanilla buttermilk cake with instant fudge frosting

This cake has a perfect crumb and is incredibly moist. It's one of those versatile recipes you can dress up or down. Here the vanilla is contrasted with an easy fudgy chocolate frosting, but you could just as well fill it with your favorite preserve and frost it with an elegant buttercream.

4 whole eggs

2 egg yolks

2 teaspoons vanilla extract

1 1/4 cups buttermilk

3 cups cake flour

2 cups sugar

4 1/2 teaspoons baking powder

1/2 teaspoon salt

2 sticks (8 ounces) unsalted butter, at room temperature

Instant Fudge Frosting (page 74)

MAKES AN 8-INCH TRIPLE-LAYER CAKE; SERVES 12 TO 16

1 Preheat the oven to 350 degrees F. Butter the bottoms and sides of three 8-inch round cake pans or spray to coat with vegetable oil. Line the bottom of each pan with a round of parchment or waxed paper and grease the paper.

2 Put the eggs and yolks in a medium mixing bowl, add the vanilla and 1/4 cup of the buttermilk. Whisk to blend well.

3 Combine the flour, sugar, baking powder, and salt in a large mixer bowl; whisk to blend. Add the butter and the remaining 1 cup buttermilk to these dry ingredients and with the mixer on low, blend together. Raise the mixer speed to medium and beat until light and fluffy, about 2 minutes.

4 Add the egg mixture in 3 additions, scraping down the sides of the bowl and mixing only until thoroughly incorporated. Divide the batter among the 3 prepared pans.

5 Bake the cake layers for 28 to 32 minutes, or until a cake tester or wooden toothpick inserted in the center comes out clean and the cake begins to pull away from the sides of the pan. Let the layers cool in the pans for 10 minutes; then carefully turn out onto wire racks, peel off the paper liners, and let cool completely.

CONTINUED

6 ounces unsweetened chocolate, melted and cooled

4 $1/2$ cups confectioners' sugar (no need to sift)

3 sticks (12 ounces) unsalted butter, at room temperature

6 tablespoons half-and-half

1 tablespoon vanilla extract

6 To assemble the cake, place one layer, flat side up, on a cake stand or serving plate. Spread $3/4$ cup of the Instant Fudge Frosting over the layer right to the edge. Repeat with the next layer. Place the last layer on top and use all but $3/4$ cup of the frosting to cover the top and sides of the cake. With an offset palette knife or spatula, smooth out the frosting all over. Place the remaining $3/4$ cup frosting in a pastry bag fitted with a medium star tube and pipe a shell border around the top and bottom edges of the cake.

instant fudge frosting   MAKES ABOUT 5 CUPS

A large food processor is the best piece of equipment to use for this frosting recipe. It whips up a perfect fudge frosting, and there is no need for a boiled syrup.

Place all of the ingredients in a food processor and pulse to incorporate. Then process until the frosting is smooth.

key west cake with mango mousse and ginger-lime cream

Seductively flavored with island ingredients, this charming cake is perfect for a lawn party or summer dinner.

6 eggs

1 cup sugar

1 teaspoon vanilla extract

1 ⅓ cups cake flour

3 tablespoons unsalted butter, melted and slightly warm

Rum Syrup (page 76)

Mango Mousse (page 76)

Ginger-Lime Cream (page 77)

MAKES AN 8-INCH TRIPLE-LAYER CAKE; SERVES 12 TO 16

1 Preheat the oven to 350 degrees F. Line the bottoms of three 8-inch round cake pans with a round of parchment or waxed paper.

2 Place the eggs in a large heatproof bowl. Gradually beat in the sugar and the vanilla. Set over a pan of simmering water and whisk constantly until all the sugar dissolves and the eggs are warmer than body temperature. Remove from the heat and, with the mixer on medium-high, whip the eggs until very fluffy and stiff enough so that a slowly dissolving ribbon forms from the dripping batter when the beaters are lifted.

3 Sift the flour and return it to the sifter. Carefully sift about a third of the flour over the top of the eggs. Using a rubber spatula, gently fold it in. Repeat with the remaining flour, folding just until blended evenly. Finally, drizzle the butter over the batter and carefully fold it in. Divide the batter among the 3 cake pans.

4 Bake the layers for 12 to 14 minutes, or until a cake tester or wooden toothpick inserted in the center comes out clean. Transfer to wire racks and let the cakes cool completely in their pans. To unmold, run a blunt knife around the rims to carefully release the edges of the cakes and tap them out gently. Carefully remove the paper on the bottom of each layer.

CONTINUED

5 To assemble the cake, place one cake layer on a cake stand or serving plate, flat side up, and soak it with $^1/_4$ cup of the Rum Syrup. Spread half of the Mango Mousse over the layer evenly. Repeat with the second cake layer, using another $^1/_4$ cup syrup and the remaining mousse. Add the last cake layer. Soak this with the last of the syrup and chill the cake for about 1 hour, to allow the mousse to set.

6 Once it's firm, frost the cake with 3 cups of the Ginger-Lime Cream. Use a pastry bag with a star tip to decorate the cake with the remaining cream. Serve each cake slice with a spoonful of the sweetened mango puree you set aside when making the mousse.

$^1/_4$ cup sugar

$^1/_2$ cup water

$^1/_4$ cup light rum

rum syrup   MAKES $^3/_4$ CUP

Combine the sugar and water in a small saucepan. Cook over medium heat, stirring to dissolve the sugar. Boil until the syrup is reduced to $^1/_2$ cup. Remove from the heat and add the rum.

2 cups diced mango, from 4 or 5 mangoes (see Baker's Note, facing page)

$^1/_3$ cup water

$^1/_3$ cup plus 1 $^1/_2$ tablespoons sugar

2 teaspoons unflavored gelatin powder

2 tablespoons light rum

1 cup heavy cream

mango mousse   MAKES ABOUT 3 CUPS

Many exotic fruits contain an enzyme that interferes with the setting action of gelatin. Cooking the mangoes before pureeing here ensures that the mousse will set up nicely.

1 Place the mango chunks in a medium nonreactive saucepan. Add the water, bring to a simmer, and cook, stirring occasionally, until soft, 10 to 15 minutes. Remove from the heat and let cool to room temperature.

2 Transfer the cooled mangoes, along with any liquid in the pan, to a blender or food processor. Puree until smooth. Remove $^1/_2$ cup of the mango puree, stir in 1 $^1/_2$ tablespoons of the sugar, and set aside for garnish. Place the remaining mango puree (about 1 cup) in a large bowl.

3 Put the gelatin in a small glass or ceramic dish. Add the rum and let soften for about 5 minutes. With a microwave on low, heat the gelatin until dissolved, 10 to 15 seconds.

4 Whisk the gelatin and remaining $1/3$ cup sugar into the mango puree until all the sugar dissolves.

5 In another large chilled bowl, whip the cream until stiff. Using a rubber spatula, fold the cream into the sweetened mango puree.

4 egg yolks

$1/2$ cup sugar

Zest of 1 lime

$1/4$ cup freshly squeezed lime juice

1 tablespoon grated fresh ginger

1 $1/2$ cups cold heavy cream

ginger-lime cream MAKES ABOUT 4 CUPS

A ginger-lime curd is blended with whipped cream to make a subtle, light frosting with a hint of the islands. Because this mixture cannot be rewhipped if it settles, make the cream shortly before frosting the cake.

1 Whisk the egg yolks in a small, heavy nonreactive sauce-pan. Gradually whisk in the sugar, then the lime zest, lime juice, and ginger. Cook over medium-low heat, stirring and scraping the bottom of the pot with a silicone or wooden spatula, until the yolks visibly thicken, 3 to 5 minutes.

2 Strain this through a fine-mesh sieve to remove the zest and ginger chunks. Cover the ginger-lime curd with plastic wrap, pressing it directly onto the surface, and refrigerate until very cold, at least 1 hour.

3 In a large mixing bowl, whip the cream until stiff. Fold the whipped cream into the ginger-lime curd.

BAKER'S NOTES

○ An easy substitute for fresh mango is refrigerated fresh mango chunks packed in light syrup, if your market carries them. If you use these, drain well before cooking.

○ Since the citrus curd for the Ginger-Lime Cream contains no starch, take care when heating the egg yolks in step 1 to avoid curdling. You can test whether the custard is ready by dragging the spoon along the bottom of the pot; when a clear path remains, remove from the heat immediately.

peach melba cake with raspberry cream

Two fruit purees—peach and raspberry—flavor the mousse filling and cream frosting of this cake, respectively. The recipes are designed to make extra of both, so that there is enough to decorate each dessert plate with a beautifully simple but dramatic technique. Best of all, the purees are made with frozen fruit, so this glorious dessert can be enjoyed year-round.

Cream Cake (page 80)

$^1/_4$ cup plus $^2/_3$ cup sugar

$^3/_4$ cup water

$^1/_4$ cup plus 2 tablespoons peach liqueur or schnapps

1 pound peaches, peeled and pitted fresh or thawed frozen with juices

1 tablespoon freshly squeezed lemon juice

1 teaspoon unflavored gelatin powder

1 cup heavy cream

Raspberry Cream (page 81)

MAKES AN 8-INCH TRIPLE-LAYER CAKE; SERVES 12 TO 16

1 Bake the Cream Cake as directed. While the cake layers are cooling, make a peach syrup by combining $^1/_4$ cup of the sugar and $^1/_2$ cup of the water in a small saucepan over medium heat. Bring to a simmer, stirring to dissolve the sugar. Continue to cook until the syrup is reduced to $^1/_2$ cup. Remove from the heat and stir in $^1/_4$ cup of the peach liqueur.

2 To make the peach mousse for the filling, combine the peaches, the remaining $^2/_3$ cup sugar, the lemon juice, and remaining $^1/_4$ cup water in a nonreactive saucepan. Bring to a boil, reduce the heat to medium-low, and simmer until the fruit is soft. Transfer to a blender and puree until smooth. Do this with great caution. A blender canister filled with hot liquid has a tendency to shoot the liquid out the top! Measure out 1 cup of peach puree and set aside for garnish. Place the remaining peach puree in a large mixing bowl.

3 Soak the gelatin in the remaining 2 tablespoons peach liqueur in a small heatproof bowl for about 5 minutes. Microwave on low for 10 to 15 seconds to heat; stir to dissolve the gelatin. Whisk into the peach puree in the large bowl.

CONTINUED

4 In a large chilled bowl, with chilled beaters, whip the cream until stiff. With a rubber spatula, fold the whipped cream into the peach puree.

5 To assemble the cake, place one cake layer, flat side up, on a cake stand or serving plate. Soak with $^1/_4$ cup of the peach syrup and spread half the peach mousse over the cake. Repeat with the second layer, using another $^1/_4$ cup syrup and the remaining mousse. Top with the last layer of cake and soak it with the last of the syrup. Cover with plastic wrap and allow the cake to chill until set, about 1 hour.

6 While the cake sets, make the Raspberry Cream. Frost the cold cake with 2 to 2 $^1/_2$ cups of the Raspberry Cream. Put the remainder in a pastry bag fitted with a large ($^3/8$-inch) star tip and pipe shells around the edge of the cake. Refrigerate, uncovered, for at least 2 hours and up to 8 hours before slicing.

7 To serve, dollop several small spoonfuls of the reserved peach and raspberry purees around the edge of each dessert plate. With a toothpick, swirl them together to create a marbled design. Place the cake slices in the center.

1 $^3/_4$ cups cake flour

3 $^3/_4$ teaspoons baking powder

$^1/_2$ teaspoon salt

1 cup heavy cream

2 teaspoons vanilla extract

1 $^1/_4$ cups sugar

2 whole eggs

2 egg yolks

3 tablespoons buttermilk

cream cake   MAKES THREE 8-INCH LAYERS

While this scrumptious cake is made with cream, it actually contains less fat than many desserts because there is no butter in the batter. These layers can be baked a day ahead; wrap well in plastic and refrigerate.

1 Preheat the oven to 350 degrees F. Butter three 8-inch round cake pans. Line the bottom of each pan with a round of parchment or waxed paper and butter the paper.

2 Sift together the flour, baking powder, and salt. Return the dry ingredients to the sifter and set aside.

3 Combine the cream and the vanilla in a large mixer bowl. With the mixer on high, whip the cream until soft peaks begin to form. Reduce the mixer speed gradually to low and beat in the sugar, but do *not* whip until stiff. Add the whole eggs and egg yolks and continue mixing until the batter forms soft peaks.

4 Sift about a third of the dry ingredients over the batter and fold in by hand. Repeat 2 more times until all of the flour mixture has been added. Finally, fold in the buttermilk. Divide the batter among the 3 prepared cake pans.

5 Bake the cake layers for 18 to 20 minutes, or until a cake tester or a wooden toothpick inserted in the center comes out clean. Allow the cakes to cool in the pans for 10 minutes, then invert them onto wire racks. Carefully peel off the paper, and allow them to cool completely.

12 ounces unsweetened frozen raspberries, thawed, with the juices

1 cup heavy cream

$1/4$ cup sugar

1 teaspoon rosewater

raspberry cream

MAKES ABOUT 3 CUPS PLUS EXTRA RASPBERRY PUREE

1 Put the raspberries and their juices in a medium non-reactive saucepan and cook over medium-low heat, mashing the berries with a large spoon, until they give up all their juices, about 15 minutes. Let cool, then puree in a blender or food processor. Strain through a sieve to remove the seeds. There will be about 1 cup raspberry puree.

2 In a chilled bowl with chilled beaters, whip the cream until stiff. Measure $1/3$ cup of the raspberry puree into another bowl. Add the sugar and rosewater and stir until the sugar dissolves. Fold in the whipped cream.

3 Sweeten the remaining raspberry puree with additional sugar to taste and use for garnish.

vanilla bean cake with white chocolate buttercream

Double vanilla—bean and extract—graces this sumptuous butter cake with an almost addictive flavor. Because only egg whites are used, it's an especially tender white cake.

3 cups cake flour

2 cups sugar

4 $^1/_2$ teaspoons baking powder

$^1/_2$ teaspoon salt

1 whole vanilla bean, split in half lengthwise (see Baker's Note, facing page)

2 sticks plus 2 tablespoons (9 ounces) unsalted butter, at room temperature

1 $^1/_3$ cups milk

5 egg whites

1 tablespoon vanilla extract

White Chocolate Buttercream (facing page)

White chocolate curls, for garnish (see page 21)

MAKES AN 8-INCH TRIPLE-LAYER CAKE; SERVES 12 TO 16

1 Preheat the oven to 350 degrees F. Butter the bottoms of three 8-inch round cake pans. Line each with a round of parchment; butter the paper.

2 Place the flour, sugar, baking powder, and salt in a large mixer bowl. With the mixer on low speed, blend well. With the tip of a small knife, scrape the tiny seeds from inside the vanilla bean into the bowl; discard the outer pod or reserve for another use. Add the butter and 1 cup of the milk and mix to blend. Raise the mixer speed to medium and beat until the batter is light and fluffy, about 2 minutes. In a mixing bowl, whisk the egg whites with the vanilla extract and the remaining $^1/_3$ cup milk. Add this to the batter in 2 to 3 additions, scraping down the bowl well and mixing only to incorporate. Divide among the 3 prepared pans.

3 Bake for about 30 minutes, or until a cake tester or wooden toothpick inserted in the center comes out clean. Allow to cool in the pans for 10 minutes; then invert onto wire racks, remove the paper, and cool completely, about 1 hour.

4 To assemble the cake, place one layer, flat side up, on a cake stand or serving plate. Spread $^2/_3$ cup of the White Chocolate Buttercream evenly over the layer. Repeat with the second layer; then top with the final layer. Using the remaining buttercream, frost the sides and top of the cake. Garnish with white chocolate curls.

3 egg whites

4 ounces good-quality white chocolate
(see Baker's Note)

1 cup sugar

¼ cup water

3 sticks (12 ounces) unsalted butter,
at room temperature

BAKER'S NOTES

○ The outer pod of the vanilla bean is
extremely aromatic, even with most
of the seeds removed. Some cooks
like to tuck the pod into a jar of sugar.
Let it stand for a week or more, and
the aroma will permeate, giving you
a batch of vanilla sugar that can be
used for baking or for custards like
crème brûlée.

○ The reason the white chocolate is
melted only halfway over heat is that
it scorches very easily. If you use a
heavy bowl, the residual heat should
melt the remaining chocolate when
you whisk it. If there are any lumps
remaining, place over simmering
water for a few more minutes.

white chocolate buttercream   MAKES ABOUT 5 CUPS

1 Put the egg whites in the bowl of an electric mixer and
set the mixer up for use. Melt the white chocolate about
halfway in a double boiler over simmering water. Remove
from the heat, stir until smooth, and set aside to cool.

2 Combine the sugar and water in a small heavy saucepan.
Set over medium heat and stir to dissolve the sugar. Bring to
a boil and cook, without stirring, until the syrup reaches the
soft-ball stage, 238 degrees F on a candy thermometer.

3 Immediately start beating the egg whites on medium-
low speed. Slowly add the syrup in a thin stream, taking care
not to hit the beaters. Continue to whip until the mixture is
body temperature and a stiff meringue has formed.

4 Reduce the speed to low and add the butter 2 to 3 tablespoons at a time. When all of the butter is incorporated,
beat on medium speed until the frosting appears to curdle.
Continue to whip, and it will suddenly come together. At this
point, add the melted white chocolate and mix well.

southern coconut cake

○ ○ ○

Coconut is a flavor people tend to love or hate. Here's a cake for those who love it. A white cake subtly flavored with coconut milk is covered with a rich, creamy frosting and drenched with loads of flaked coconut. It's a white-on-white creation that will look perfect on the frilliest of tables.

5 egg whites

1/2 cup milk

2 teaspoons vanilla extract

3 cups cake flour

2 1/3 cups sugar

4 1/2 teaspoons baking powder

1/2 teaspoon salt

2 sticks (8 ounces) unsalted butter, at warm room temperature

1 cup unsweetened coconut milk

Cream Cheese Buttercream Frosting (page 87)

2 1/2 cups sweetened flaked coconut

MAKES AN 8-INCH TRIPLE-LAYER CAKE; SERVES 12 TO 16

1 Preheat the oven to 350 degrees F. Butter the bottoms of three 8-inch round cake pans or coat with vegetable cooking spray. Line the bottom of each pan with a round of parchment or waxed paper and butter the paper.

2 Put the egg whites in a mixing bowl and whisk slightly. Add the 1/2 cup milk and the vanilla and whisk to mix thoroughly; set aside.

3 In a large mixer bowl, combine the flour, sugar, baking powder, and salt. With the mixer on low, beat to mix well and break up any lumps, about 30 seconds. Add the butter and coconut milk and, with the mixer still on low, beat to combine. Raise the speed to medium and beat until light and fluffy, about 2 minutes.

4 Add the egg white mixture in 2 or 3 additions, scraping down the sides of the bowl and mixing just long enough to incorporate between additions. Divide the batter among the 3 prepared pans.

5 Bake for 30 minutes, or until a cake tester or wooden toothpick inserted in the center comes out clean. Allow the cakes to cool in their pans for 10 minutes. Then turn them out onto cooling racks and allow to cool completely.

CONTINUED

6 To decorate the cake, place one layer, flat side up, on an 8-inch cake board. Cover this layer with 1 cup of the buttercream frosting, spreading it evenly right to the edge. Sprinkle $1/2$ cup coconut over the frosting. Add the second layer of cake and repeat with another 1 cup frosting and $1/2$ cup coconut. Top with the final layer of cake and frost the top and sides with the remaining frosting.

7 Place the remaining $1 1/2$ cups coconut on a large baking tray. Pick up the cake and hold it on the palm of one hand over the tray. Using the other hand, scoop up some of the coconut and press it onto the side of the cake. Continue to do this, rotating the cake slightly each time, until the sides are completely coated. Set the cake on a serving plate and sprinkle any remaining coconut over the top. Chill for at least 1 hour to allow the frosting to firm up before slicing.

12 ounces cream cheese,
slightly chilled

1 stick plus 6 tablespoons (7 ounces)
unsalted butter, at room temperature

1 cup confectioners' sugar,
sifted after measuring

2 teaspoons vanilla extract

1 cup granulated sugar

$\frac{1}{4}$ cup water

3 egg whites

cream cheese buttercream frosting
MAKES ABOUT 5 CUPS

Everyone loves the unctuousness of cream cheese frosting, but the silky texture of buttercream is irresistible. Unfortunately, if you try to make a buttercream with cream cheese, it breaks. This technique solves the problem perfectly, giving you the best of both frostings.

1 Place the cream cheese in a mixer bowl and beat on medium speed until slightly fluffy and smooth. Add the butter 1 to 2 tablespoons at a time, mixing until smooth. Add the confectioners' sugar and vanilla and mix until fluffy. Set this aside at room temperature while the buttercream is prepared.

2 To prepare the buttercream, combine the granulated sugar and water in a small heavy saucepan and bring to a boil over medium heat, stirring to dissolve the sugar. Continue to cook, without stirring, until the syrup reaches the soft-ball stage, 238 degrees F on a candy thermometer.

3 Meanwhile, put the egg whites in a mixer bowl and have the mixer set up and ready to go. When the syrup is ready, turn the mixer to medium-low and begin mixing the egg whites. Slowly add the hot syrup to the whites, taking care not to pour it directly onto the beaters, or it may splash. When all of the syrup is incorporated, raise the speed to medium-high and beat until the egg white mixture has cooled to body temperature and a stiff meringue forms.

4 With the mixer on low speed, begin adding the cream cheese mixture by the spoonful. When all is incorporated, raise the speed to medium and whip until the frosting is smooth and fluffy.

sky-high strawberry shortcake

○○○

5 tablespoons unsalted butter,
at room temperature

3/4 cup plus 2 tablespoons sugar

1 teaspoon vanilla extract

2 eggs

1 1/2 cups cake flour

2 1/2 teaspoons baking powder
(see Baker's Note)

1/4 teaspoon salt

2/3 cup buttermilk

1 1/2 cups heavy cream

Fresh Strawberry Filling (page 90)

Whole strawberries, for garnish
(see Baker's Note)

BAKER'S NOTES

○ It is a little unusual to use all baking
powder and no baking soda in a cake
that contains buttermilk. It was
done on purpose here to emphasize
the nuttiness of the buttermilk and
employ the acid to produce an extra-
tender crumb.

○ For decoration, choose regularly shaped
whole berries that have not been
hulled. Halve them right through the
green tops down to the pointed
bottoms, creating small red hearts
topped with green. Place them around

continued

Fresh strawberries sweetened and flavored with a blend of vanilla and rosewater or anisette impart an almost floral taste to this buttery cake. Mounds of lightly sweetened whipped cream fill the layers and top the cake, resulting in a heady richness and plenty of moisture.

MAKES A 6-INCH TRIPLE-LAYER CAKE; SERVES 8 TO 10

1 Preheat the oven to 350 degrees F. Grease the bottoms and sides of three 6-inch round cake pans. Line the bottom of each with a round of parchment or waxed paper; grease the paper.

2 In a large mixer bowl, cream the butter, 3/4 cup of the sugar, and the vanilla with an electric mixer until light and fluffy. Add the eggs one at a time, scraping down the sides of the bowl well after each addition.

3 Sift together the flour, baking powder, and salt. Add these dry ingredients to the batter, alternating with the buttermilk in 2 or 3 additions. Divide the batter among the 3 prepared cake pans.

4 Bake the cake layers for 20 to 25 minutes, or until a cake tester or wooden toothpick inserted in the center comes out clean. Allow to cool in the pans for 10 minutes; then invert onto wire racks, carefully peel off the paper, and allow to cool completely.

5 In a large chilled bowl with chilled beaters, whip the cream with the remaining 2 tablespoons sugar until stiff. There will be about 3 cups.

CONTINUED

the top of the cake with the cut sides facing up.

o While the cake layers can be baked up to 2 days in advance, if wrapped well and refrigerated, the finished shortcake will not hold up for more than a day. However, for best texture and flavor, it's important to assemble the dessert completely at least 2 hours in advance so that the juices and cream have a chance to seep into the cake layers and all the flavors meld beautifully.

2 pints strawberries, small if possible

2 teaspoons rosewater or
2 tablespoons anisette liqueur

2 teaspoons vanilla extract

1/2 cup sugar

6 To assemble the strawberry shortcake, place one cake layer, flat side up, on a small cake stand or a serving plate. Top with 3/4 cup of the Fresh Strawberry Filling, spooning it over the entire layer and making sure any juices go onto the cake layer and not the plate, if possible. Top this with 1 cup of the whipped cream, spreading it evenly over the berries. Repeat with the second cake layer and another 3/4 cup filling and 1 cup whipped cream. Top with the final cake layer flat side up. Cover with the last of the whipped cream and garnish with a few whole berries. For best flavor, cover the dessert with a cake dome or loose plastic wrap and refrigerate for about 2 hours before slicing. Serve with the remaining Fresh Strawberry Filling on the side.

fresh strawberry filling   MAKES ABOUT 2 1/2 CUPS

If you have a choice when buying your strawberries, choose berries that are darker red. In general, this signifies they are riper, which means they will yield more juice and will be sweeter and more intense in flavor.

Clean and hull the berries and slice into pieces about the thickness of a nickel. Place in a bowl and add the rosewater or liqueur, vanilla, and sugar. Stir to coat them, cover the bowl, and let the berries macerate at room temperature until they exude their juices, about 1 hour.

the fabulous lady b cake

Modeled after the Southern confection dubbed Lady Baltimore cake, which ostensibly originated in the late nineteenth century either in a bakery in Baltimore or in a teahouse in South Carolina, this recipe takes the original and runs with it—right into the twenty-first century. Angel food layers take the place of butter cake, a lemony fig filling replaces the traditional raisin conserve, and the sticky-sweet boiled marshmallow frosting has been transformed into a sherry buttercream. Oh, my!

Angel Food Cake (page 92)

¹/₂ cup walnut halves

Sherry Buttercream (page 93)

3 tablespoons finely chopped moist dried figs

1 teaspoon grated orange zest

¹/₂ teaspoon grated lemon zest

MAKES A 6-INCH TRIPLE-LAYER CAKE; SERVES 8 TO 10

1 Bake the Angel Food Cake as directed. When the layers come out, leave the oven on. Spread out the walnuts in a small baking pan and toast in the oven until fragrant and lightly browned, 6 to 8 minutes. Transfer to a dish and let cool. Finely chop half the walnuts; set the remaining halves aside for decoration.

2 While the cake layers are cooling, make the Sherry Buttercream.

3 To make the filling, in a bowl, combine the chopped walnuts and figs with the grated orange and lemon zests. Add ¹/₂ cup of the buttercream and mix well.

4 To assemble the cake, place one layer on a small cake stand or serving plate, flat side up. Spread half of the filling over the top, leaving a ¹/₄-inch margin around the edge. Add the second layer and cover with the remaining filling. Set the third layer on top and frost the entire cake with the remaining buttercream. Decorate with the toasted walnut halves.

CONTINUED

6 egg whites

²/₃ cup granulated sugar

¹/₂ teaspoon cream of tartar

1 teaspoon vanilla extract

²/₃ cup cake flour

²/₃ cup confectioners' sugar

¹/₄ teaspoon salt

BAKER'S NOTE

Angel food cake does not hold up over time; it becomes soft and sticky. So do not refrigerate this cake, and plan to serve it the same day it is made.

angel food cake   MAKES THREE 6-INCH LAYERS

Angel food cake is often baked in tall tube pans, but here it is treated like a layer cake. If you want to use this recipe sometime for a more traditional cake, you could bake it in a 6-cup tube pan.

1 Preheat the oven to 325 degrees F. This recipe requires three 6-inch round cake pans; do not grease them.

2 With an electric mixer fitted with the whip attachment on medium-high speed, whip the egg whites in a mixer bowl until frothy. Slowly add the granulated sugar and the cream of tartar and continue to beat until soft peaks form. Do not whip the meringue until stiff, or the cake will have a dry, dense crumb. Mix in the vanilla.

3 Sift together the flour, confectioners' sugar, and salt. Return to the sifter and dust about a third of the dry ingredients over the meringue. Fold in thoroughly but gently. Repeat 2 more times. Gently divide the batter among the 3 pans, being careful not to deflate it and spreading it smooth on top with a rubber spatula.

4 Bake for about 25 minutes, or until a cake tester or wooden toothpick inserted in the center comes out clean. Invert the pans over cooling racks and allow them to cool completely in this position. To unmold, run a blunt knife around the edge of the pan to release the cake.

3 egg whites

1 cup sugar

1/4 cup plus 2 tablespoons dry sherry

2 sticks plus 2 tablespoons
(9 ounces) unsalted butter, at warm
room temperature

sherry buttercream   MAKES ABOUT 4 CUPS

1 Put the egg whites in a mixer bowl and set the electric mixer up for use with the whip attachment.

2 Combine the sugar and 1/4 cup of the sherry in a small heavy saucepan. Bring to a simmer, stirring to dissolve the sugar. Continue to cook, without stirring, washing down any sugar crystals from the sides of the pan with a wet pastry brush, until the syrup reaches the soft-ball stage, 238 degrees F.

3 With the mixer on medium-low, whip the egg whites until frothy. Gradually pour in the syrup in a thin stream, taking care not to hit the whip. Continue to beat until the mixture cools to body temperature and forms a stiff meringue.

4 Reduce the speed to low and add the softened butter 1 to 2 tablespoons at a time. Return to medium speed and whip until fluffy and smooth. The buttercream will appear to curdle just before this point, then it will suddenly come together. Beat in the remaining 2 tablespoons sherry.

triple-decker boston cream pie

While some people prefer chocolate and others opt for vanilla, this version of the American classic offers the best of both worlds. As anyone who has ever dipped a fork into a wedge of the luscious dessert knows, Boston cream pie isn't a pie at all. It's a vanilla sponge cake filled with rich vanilla pudding.

The original was topped simply with a shower of confectioners' sugar. Then in 1855, a French pastry chef hired to develop desserts for the newly opened Parker House in Boston added an intense bittersweet glaze, which dripped down the side like chocolate icicles. That is the version given here—in three layers, of course.

2 cups cake flour

2 teaspoons baking powder

1 1/2 cups sugar

8 eggs, separated

1 tablespoon fresh lemon juice

6 tablespoons vegetable oil

2 teaspoons vanilla extract

Vanilla Custard (page 96)

Chocolate Glaze (page 97)

MAKES A 9-INCH TRIPLE-LAYER CAKE; SERVES 16 TO 20

1 Preheat the oven to 350 degrees F. Line the bottoms of three 9-inch round cake pans with a round of parchment or waxed paper.

2 Sift together the cake flour, baking powder, and 1/2 cup of the sugar. Set these dry ingredients aside.

3 In a medium mixing bowl, whisk together the egg yolks, lemon juice, oil, and vanilla until blended.

4 In a large clean mixer bowl, beat the egg whites with an electric mixer on high speed until foamy. Gradually add the remaining 1 cup sugar and continue beating until moderately stiff peaks form that droop slightly.

5 Mix a quarter of the whipped whites into the yolks, then carefully and gently fold the yolk mixture back into the remaining whites without overmixing. Now sift about a third of the dry ingredients over the egg mixture and carefully fold in. Repeat this step in 2 more additions. You don't want to deflate the batter by handling it roughly or by dumping a large quantity of flour into the batter all at once. Divide the batter among the 3 prepared cake pans.

CONTINUED

2 tablespoons cornstarch

2 cups whole milk

6 egg yolks

3/4 cup sugar

2 teaspoons vanilla extract

6 Bake for 15 to 20 minutes, or until a cake tester or wooden toothpick stuck into the center of each layer comes out clean and the cake springs back when touched lightly. Let the layers cool completely in their pans on wire racks. To unmold, gently run a blunt knife around the edges of each pan, then invert to turn out the cakes. Carefully peel off the paper liners.

7 To assemble the cake, put one layer, flat side up, on a cake stand or serving plate. Spread half the Vanilla Custard over it, smoothing the filling right out to the edge of the layer. Repeat with the second layer. Place the third layer on top and pour the Chocolate Glaze over the top of the cake, smoothing and spreading so that the glaze drips down the sides of the cake.

vanilla custard   MAKES ABOUT 2 1/2 CUPS

The "cream" in Boston cream pie is actually a boiled custard. Rich and lush on the tongue, it's the contrast between this golden vanilla custard and the dark chocolate glaze, much like the flavors of an éclair, that give this dessert it's irresistible quality.

1 In a large heatproof bowl, combine the cornstarch and 1/4 cup of the milk. Stir until smooth and free of any lumps. Whisk in the egg yolks and set aside on top of a pot holder to anchor the bowl as close to your stove as possible.

2 In a medium stainless steel or enameled saucepan, combine the remaining 1 3/4 cups milk and the sugar. Bring to a boil over medium heat, stirring to dissolve the sugar. (Watch carefully, because the liquid can bubble up quickly.)

3 Ladle about one-third of the hot sweetened milk into the egg yolk mixture in a thin stream, whisking constantly. Gradually whisk this egg yolk mixture into the remaining hot milk in the pan. Whisking constantly, bring just to a boil. Reduce the heat to low and boil gently, still whisking constantly, for 1 minute.

4 Transfer the custard to a bowl and whisk in the vanilla. Let cool slightly. Cover with plastic wrap, pressing it directly onto the surface of the custard to prevent a skin from forming. Refrigerate until chilled.

¹⁄₄ cup half-and-half

2 tablespoons light corn syrup

1 cup bittersweet or semisweet chocolate (about 6 ounces), in small pieces

chocolate glaze MAKES ABOUT 1 CUP

In a small heavy saucepan, combine the half-and-half and corn syrup. Bring to a simmer over moderately low heat, stirring to blend. Remove from the heat, add the chocolate, and let stand for 1 minute. Whisk until smooth.

fruit-flavored cakes

apricot carrot cake

Everyone loves this cake, which boasts tart dried apricots and pine-apple in place of the usual raisins, making it a little less sweet and more complex. Another switch is the addition of toasted walnut oil instead of walnuts, for a very subtle nutty taste.

A generous amount of Cream Cheese Frosting lends itself to decorative swirls. Dried apricots, cut in half, and pineapple chips or toasted walnut halves can also be used for garnish.

3 eggs

2 cups sugar

1/4 cup honey

1 cup walnut oil (see Baker's Note)

2 teaspoons grated fresh ginger (see Baker's Note)

2 cups finely shredded carrots

1/2 cup dried apricots, finely chopped

1/2 cup crushed unsweetened pineapple, well drained

1 cup sweetened flaked coconut

2 cups plus 2 tablespoons all-purpose flour

2 teaspoons ground cinnamon

2 teaspoons baking soda

1/2 teaspoon salt

3/4 cup tangerine or orange marmalade

Cream Cheese Frosting (recipe follows)

MAKES A 9-INCH TRIPLE-LAYER CAKE; SERVES 16 TO 20

1 Preheat the oven to 350 degrees F. Butter three 9-inch round cake pans. Line the bottom of each pan with a round of parchment or waxed paper and butter the paper. Dust with flour; tap out any excess.

2 In a large mixing bowl, whisk the eggs lightly. Gradually beat in the sugar until blended. Beat in the honey, walnut oil, and ginger until well blended. Add the carrots, dried apricots, pineapple, and coconut and mix well.

3 In 2 additions, sift the flour, cinnamon, baking soda, and salt right onto the batter and fold it in. Divide among the prepared cake pans.

4 Bake for 25 to 30 minutes, or until a cake tester or wooden toothpick stuck into the center of each layer comes out moist, with a few crumbs clinging to it. Let the cakes cool completely in the pans on wire racks and run a blunt knife around the edges before unmolding. This is a tender cake that will not come out of the pan easily when hot. After turning out the layers, carefully peel off the paper. Spread about 3 tablespoons marmalade thinly and evenly over the flat side of each layer. Chill the layers for several hours before frosting the cake; the layers firm up and are easier to work with when cool.

o This recipe was tested using a California toasted walnut oil, which was very fragrant. Alternatively, you could use a good French cold-pressed walnut oil.

o When preparing grated ginger, one of the ingredients in this cake, keep in mind the fibers run parallel to its length. So you want to grate or slice ginger across the grain, cutting those fibers short as you go along.

8 ounces cream cheese, at room temperature

1 stick (4 ounces) unsalted butter, at room temperature

4 cups confectioners' sugar

1 $\frac{1}{2}$ teaspoons vanilla extract

5 To assemble the cake, place one of the cold layers, marmalade side up, on a cake stand or serving plate and spread approximately $\frac{1}{2}$ cup of Cream Cheese Frosting evenly over the marmalade all the way to the edge of the cake. Place a second layer, marmalade side up, on top of the first and cover with another $\frac{1}{2}$ cup frosting. Finally, set the third layer in place, marmalade side up once again, and use the remaining frosting to cover the top and sides of the cake, swirling decoratively.

cream cheese frosting   MAKES ABOUT 3 CUPS

1 Put the cream cheese and butter into a food processor and process until smooth and well blended.

2 Add half the confectioners' sugar and pulse to incorporate. Repeat with the remaining sugar and the vanilla, then process until the frosting is smooth and glossy.

banana–chocolate chip cake

What is not to love about this tall beauty? A sweetly spiced banana cake, studded with chocolate chips, is filled and topped with fresh banana slices, a rum-flavored caramel drizzle, and whipped cream. Count on everyone to request seconds.

2 1/4 cups cake flour

1 1/3 cups plus 3 tablespoons sugar

1 1/4 teaspoons baking powder

1 1/4 teaspoons baking soda

1 teaspoon ground cinnamon

1 teaspoon Chinese five-spice powder (see Baker's Note, page 104)

1/2 teaspoon salt

1 stick (4 ounces) plus 1 tablespoon unsalted butter, at room temperature

1 cup mashed very ripe bananas, plus 2 ripe but firm bananas, thinly sliced (see Baker's Note, page 104)

3 eggs

3/4 cup buttermilk

1 1/2 teaspoons vanilla extract

3/4 cup mini semisweet chocolate chips, plus more for decoration

1 1/2 cups heavy cream

Caramel Drizzle (page 104)

MAKES AN 8-INCH TRIPLE-LAYER CAKE; SERVES 12 TO 16

1 Preheat the oven to 350 degrees F. Butter the bottoms of three 8-inch round cake pans or coat with vegetable cooking spray. Line the bottom of each pan with a round of parchment or waxed paper and butter the paper.

2 Place the flour, 1 1/3 cups sugar, baking powder, baking soda, cinnamon, five-spice powder, and salt in a large mixing bowl. With an electric mixer on low, blend well, about 1 minute. Add the butter and mashed bananas and beat until well blended. Raise the mixer speed to medium and beat until light and fluffy, about 3 minutes.

3 Combine the eggs, buttermilk, and vanilla in a small bowl and whisk to blend. Add to the batter in 3 additions, scraping the bowl well and beating just until blended after each addition. Finally, fold in half of the chocolate chips by hand. Divide the batter among the 3 prepared cake pans. Sprinkle the remaining chocolate chips on top.

4 Bake the cake layers for 25 to 28 minutes, or until a cake tester or wooden toothpick inserted in the center comes out clean. Let cool in the pans for 10 to 15 minutes, then invert to unmold onto wire racks. Carefully peel off the paper liners and let cool completely before filling and frosting.

5 For the filling and topping, in a large chilled bowl with chilled beaters, whip the cream with the remaining 3 tablespoons sugar until stiff.

CONTINUED

**1 cup prepared thick caramel sauce,
such as *cajeta* (see page 171)**

3 tablespoons dark rum

6 To assemble the cake, place one layer, flat side up, on a
cake stand or serving plate. Top with 2 to 3 tablespoons of
the Caramel Drizzle and spread it thinly but evenly over the
whole layer. Arrange about half the banana slices on top in
a single layer. Cover the bananas with 1 cup of the whipped
cream, spreading it evenly over the layer. Repeat with the
second layer, adding more caramel, bananas, and cream.
Place the final cake layer on top and coat it with 2 to 3
tablespoons of caramel; reserve the remaining caramel to
serve with the cake slices. Top with the remaining whipped
cream and spread it evenly over the entire layer. Decorate
the top with chocolate chips and a few more banana slices,
if you like.

caramel drizzle   MAKES ABOUT 1 1/4 CUPS

Put the caramel sauce in a small heavy saucepan and
warm over low heat, stirring, just until heated through,
about 2 minutes. Remove from the heat and whisk in
the rum. Let cool to room temperature before using.

banana cake with praline filling and white chocolate ganache

You're in for a delightful surprise here as a modicum of ripe banana subtly flavors a light white cake without overpowering it. Sugared pecans go in the praline filling and garnish the top of the cake.

3 cups cake flour

3 1/2 teaspoons baking powder

1 1/2 teaspoons ground cinnamon

1/2 teaspoon salt

3/4 cup milk

1/2 cup mashed ripe bananas (see Baker's Note)

2 sticks (8 ounces) unsalted butter, at room temperature

2 cups sugar

7 egg whites

Praline Filling (page 106)

White Chocolate Ganache (page 107)

Sugared Pecans (page 106), for garnish

BAKER'S NOTE

For a rich banana flavor, make sure the banana you use is well ripened, with a peel that's covered with freckles and is turning brown.

MAKES A 9-INCH TRIPLE-LAYER CAKE; SERVES 16 TO 20

1 Preheat the oven to 350 degrees F. Butter three 9-inch round cake pans. Line the bottom of each with a round of parchment or waxed paper and butter the paper.

2 Sift together the flour, baking powder, cinnamon, and salt. Set the dry ingredients aside. In a food processor or blender, process the milk and mashed banana into a smooth, light puree.

3 In a large bowl, cream the butter and sugar with an electric mixer until light and fluffy. On medium-high speed, beat in the egg whites 2 or 3 at a time until smooth, scraping down the sides of the bowl between additions.

4 With the mixer on low speed, add the dry ingredients and banana puree alternately in 2 or 3 additions, beating until just blended between additions. Scrape down the sides of the bowl and beat on medium-high speed for 1 minute. Divide the batter among the 3 prepared cake pans.

5 Bake for 20 to 25 minutes, or until a cake tester or wooden toothpick stuck into the center of each layer comes out clean and the cake is beginning to pull away from the sides of the pan. Let the layers cool in their pans for 10 minutes. Then turn out onto wire racks, gently peel off the paper liners, and let cool completely, at least 1 hour.

CONTINUED

6 To assemble the cake, put one layer, flat side up, on a cake stand or serving plate. Cover the top evenly with half of the Praline Filling, leaving a $1/4$-inch margin around the edges. Place the second layer on top, again flat side up, and cover it with the remaining filling. Finally, add the third cake layer and frost the top and sides of the cake with the White Chocolate Ganache. Garnish with Sugared Pecans.

1 cup Sugared Pecans, completely cooled (recipe follows)

1 $1/2$ cups White Chocolate Ganache (facing page)

praline filling MAKES ABOUT 2 $1/4$ CUPS

1 With a large chef's knife, chop the pecans. Or pulse in a food processor, being careful not to grind to a paste.

2 Add the chopped sugared pecans to the White Chocolate Ganache and stir to mix well.

1 $1/2$ cups pecan halves

3 cups vegetable oil

1 cup confectioners' sugar

sugared pecans MAKES 1 $1/2$ CUPS

This rather unusual technique is based on spiced nuts we make at the Loveless Cafe. Those have cayenne added for a hit of heat. Plain or hot, they're irresistible for snacking or salads, and hard to beat when they're still warm.

The nuts can be prepared 2 or 3 days ahead of time and stored in a tightly closed container. For frying, it's always best to choose a bland vegetable oil with a high smoke point, such as peanut, canola, soybean, or sunflower.

1 Place the pecans in a medium saucepan, add water to cover, and heat to boiling. Boil the pecans slowly until they're swollen and soft, 5 to 8 minutes. Drain the nuts well in a sieve for about 5 minutes. (Do not pat dry; the nuts must remain damp.)

2 While the nuts are draining, heat the oil in a large heavy saucepan or deep fat fryer to 350 degrees F.

3 Set half the nuts aside. Dust the remaining nuts in the sieve with $1/2$ cup of the confectioners' sugar. Shake the sieve to coat the nuts evenly, letting any excess sugar fall away. Immediately add the coated nuts to the hot oil. Fry until they're a light golden brown, 2 to 3 minutes. Using a slotted spoon, scoop the nuts out of the oil and drain them on several thicknesses of paper towels. Repeat with the remaining pecans and confectioners' sugar.

8 ounces white chocolate, chopped

2 $1/2$ cups heavy cream

1 $1/2$ teaspoons vanilla extract

white chocolate ganache   MAKES ABOUT 4 CUPS

1 Put the white chocolate in a medium heatproof bowl. In a small saucepan, bring $1/2$ cup of the cream to a boil. Pour the hot cream over the chocolate. Let stand for 1 minute, then whisk until smooth. Let the white chocolate cream stand until cooled to room temperature.

2 In a chilled bowl with chilled beaters, beat the remaining 2 cups cream and the vanilla until softly whipped. Stir in the white chocolate cream and beat until fairly stiff, taking care not to overbeat the mixture, which would cause the ganache to separate.

marbled lemon-blueberry butter cake

Blueberries and lemon make a sublime pairing, and here the two are doubly matched. An easy, homemade blueberry preserve is flavored with both lemon juice and lemon zest, as well as a touch of fresh ginger to enliven the mix. Then the preserve is used twice: swirled through a lemon-flavored batter, for a gorgeous lavender-and-yellow marbled cake, and used to fill the layers. Be sure to make the preserves before you begin the cake.

2 sticks (8 ounces) unsalted butter, at room temperature

2 cups sugar

2 teaspoons grated lemon zest

1 1/2 teaspoons lemon extract

7 egg whites

3 cups cake flour

4 teaspoons baking powder

1/2 teaspoon salt

1 1/4 cups milk

Lemon-Blueberry Preserves (page 110)

Lemon Buttercream Frosting (page 111)

Fresh blueberries, for decoration

MAKES AN 8-INCH TRIPLE-LAYER CAKE; SERVES 16 TO 20

1 Preheat the oven to 350 degrees F. Butter the bottom and sides of three 8-inch round cake pans. Line the bottom of each pan with a round of parchment or waxed paper and butter the paper.

2 In a mixer bowl, cream the butter, sugar, lemon zest, and lemon extract until light and fluffy. Gradually add the egg whites 2 or 3 at a time, beating well between additions and stopping occasionally to scrape down the sides of the bowl.

3 Combine the flour, baking powder, and salt; whisk gently to blend. In 2 or 3 alternating additions, beat the dry ingredients and milk into the butter mixture, scraping down the sides of the bowl several times. Beat on medium-high speed for about 1 minute to smooth out any lumps and aerate the batter.

4 Scoop 1 cup of the batter into a small bowl. Divide the remainder equally among the 3 prepared cake pans, smoothing the tops with a rubber spatula. This gives you a "clean canvas" to work with. Add 2 1/2 tablespoons of the Lemon-Blueberry Preserves to the reserved batter and blend well. Drizzle heaping teaspoons of this blueberry mixture over the batter in the pans. Using a skewer or paring knife, swirl the blueberry mixture in short strokes to drag it down through the lemon batter without mixing it in.

CONTINUED

5 Bake for about 25 minutes, or until a cake tester or wooden toothpick stuck into the center comes out clean and the cake begins to pull away from the sides of the pan. Let the layers cool in their pans for about 10 minutes, then turn out onto wire racks, carefully peel off the paper liners, and let cool completely, at least 1 hour.

6 To assemble the cake, place a layer, flat side up, on a cake stand or serving plate. Spread half of the Lemon-Blueberry Preserves over the top. Place a second layer on top of the first and spread the remaining preserves over it. Finally, place the third layer on top of the second and frost the sides and top of the cake with the Lemon Buttercream Frosting. Decorate with fresh blueberries.

3 cups blueberries, fresh or frozen

3/4 cup sugar

2 tablespoons freshly squeezed lemon juice

1 1/2 teaspoons grated lemon zest

1 teaspoon grated fresh ginger

lemon-blueberry preserves   MAKES ABOUT 1 CUP

This luscious jam can be made up to 5 days in advance and refrigerated. If using frozen berries, measure them while frozen, then thaw completely in a bowl, saving any juices, before proceeding with the recipe.

1 Puree the blueberries with any juices they have exuded in a blender or food processor. Pass the puree through a coarse strainer or the medium disk of a food mill to remove the skins.

2 In a heavy medium nonreactive saucepan, combine the blueberry puree with the sugar, lemon juice, lemon zest, and ginger. Bring to a gentle boil over medium heat, stirring frequently to dissolve the sugar. Continue cooking, stirring often, for 20 minutes, until the preserves have thickened and are reduced to 1 cup. To check for proper thickness, place 1 to 2 teaspoons on a small china or glass plate and put it in the freezer until cold. Drag your finger through the thickened puree: a clear path should remain. If it's not ready, cook 5 minutes longer and repeat the test. Let the preserves cool, then cover and refrigerate for up to 5 days.

1 cup sugar

¼ cup water

2 eggs

3 sticks (12 ounces) unsalted butter, at room temperature

2 tablespoons freshly squeezed lemon juice

lemon buttercream frosting MAKES ABOUT 3 ½ CUPS

1 In a small nonreactive saucepan, combine the sugar and water. Bring to a boil over medium heat, stirring to dissolve the sugar. Continue to boil without stirring, occasionally washing down the sides of the pan with a wet pastry brush, until the syrup reaches the soft-ball stage, 238 degrees F on a candy thermometer. Immediately remove from the heat.

2 In a large mixer bowl with an electric mixer on medium speed, beat the eggs briefly. Slowly add the hot syrup in a thin stream, pouring it down the sides of the bowl; be careful to avoid hitting the beaters, or the syrup may splatter. When all the syrup has been added, raise the speed to medium-high and beat until the mixture is very fluffy and cooled to body temperature. This can take 15 to 20 minutes.

3 Reduce the mixer speed to medium-low and gradually add the softened butter 2 to 3 tablespoons at a time, beating well between additions. As you're adding the last few tablespoons of butter, the frosting will appear to break, then suddenly come together like whipped butter. Beat in the lemon juice, and the frosting is ready for use.

triple lemon chiffon cake

○ ○ ○

Light lemon layers, Rich Lemon Curd filling, and Lemon Cream Frosting add up to a tart-sweet cake that will brighten any dessert lover's day.

8 eggs, separated

1/4 cup walnut oil

2 tablespoons freshly squeezed lemon juice

1 tablespoon grated lemon zest

1/3 cup water

1/2 teaspoon cream of tartar

1 1/2 cups sugar

1 3/4 cups cake flour

1/2 teaspoon baking soda

1/2 teaspoon salt

Rich Lemon Curd (facing page)

Lemon Cream Frosting (facing page)

MAKES A 9-INCH TRIPLE-LAYER CAKE; SERVES 16 TO 20

1 Preheat the oven to 350 degrees F. Line the bottoms of three 9-inch cake pans with rounds of parchment or waxed paper but do not grease the pans.

2 In a medium-large bowl, whisk together the egg yolks, walnut oil, lemon juice, lemon zest, and water.

3 In a large mixer bowl, whip the egg whites with the cream of tartar on medium speed until frothy. Gradually add 1/2 cup of the sugar and continue to beat until soft peaks form.

4 Sift the flour, remaining 1 cup sugar, baking soda, and salt into a very large bowl. Whisk gently to combine. Make a well in the center, pour in the egg yolk mixture, and stir to make a smooth paste. Add one-fourth of the beaten egg whites and fold in to lighten the batter. Fold in the remaining whites. Divide the batter among the 3 prepared pans.

5 Bake for about 16 minutes, or until a cake tester or wooden toothpick inserted in the center comes out clean. Transfer to wire racks and let the cakes cool completely in their pans. To unmold, run a blunt knife around the edges to release. Invert to unmold; carefully peel off the paper liners.

6 To assemble the cake, place one layer on a cake stand or serving plate. Top with a heaping 1/4 cup of the Rich Lemon Curd, and spread it out evenly. Repeat with the next layer and finally add the third layer. Frost the top and sides with the Lemon Cream Frosting.

rich lemon curd   MAKES ABOUT 1 CUP

3 whole eggs

2 egg yolks

1/2 cup sugar

1/2 cup plus 1 tablespoon freshly squeezed lemon juice (from about 4 lemons)

Grated zest of 3 lemons

4 tablespoons unsalted butter, at room temperature

Note that while most of this curd is used to fill the cake, 3 tablespoons should be reserved to flavor the frosting.

Whisk together the whole eggs, egg yolks, sugar, lemon juice, and lemon zest in a medium bowl. Transfer to a small heavy nonreactive saucepan. Gently heat the mixture, whisking until it thickens enough to coat a spoon; do not boil. Pour this mixture through a wire mesh strainer into a heatproof dish (this catches all of the rubbery parts of the egg whites and removes the zest). Stir in the butter and cover the curd with plastic wrap, pressing it to the surface to prevent a skin from forming. Refrigerate it until needed.

lemon cream frosting   MAKES ABOUT 3 1/4 CUPS

1 1/2 cups heavy cream

2 tablespoons sugar

3 tablespoons Rich Lemon Curd (recipe above)

Whip the cream with the sugar in a large chilled bowl with chilled beaters until somewhat stiff peaks form. Be careful not to fully whip at this point because the curd will need to be folded in. Fold in the lemon curd, forming a stiff frosting.

orange–grand marnier cake

Here's a chiffon cake that's given a triple boost of flavor from grated orange zest, fresh orange juice, and a generous splash of Grand Marnier syrup. If blood oranges are available, they make an interesting variation.

1 3/4 cups cake flour

1 1/2 cups sugar

1/2 teaspoon baking soda

1/2 teaspoon salt

1/4 cup neutral vegetable oil, such as canola, soybean, or vegetable blend

8 eggs, separated

2 tablespoons freshly squeezed orange juice

1 tablespoon grated orange zest

1/3 cup water

1/2 teaspoon cream of tartar

Grand Marnier Syrup (facing page)

Orange–Grand Marnier Frosting (facing page)

Candied orange peel and white chocolate shavings, for decoration

MAKES A 9-INCH TRIPLE-LAYER CAKE; SERVES 16 TO 20

1 Preheat the oven to 350 degrees F. Line the bottoms of three 9-inch round cake pans with parchment or waxed paper but do not grease the pans.

2 Sift the flour, 1 cup of the sugar, the baking soda, and salt into a large bowl; stir to blend. Whisk in the oil, egg yolks, orange juice, orange zest, and water until well blended.

3 Put the egg whites in a clean large mixer bowl with the cream of tartar and, using the whip attachment of an electric mixer, beat until frothy. Slowly add the remaining 1/2 cup sugar and whip until soft peaks form. Do not overbeat or the cake will be dry.

4 Add one-fourth of the beaten whites to the cake batter and fold them in to lighten the batter. Gently fold in the remaining whites just until no streaks remain. Divide the batter among the 3 prepared pans.

5 Bake the cake layers for 16 to 18 minutes, or until a cake tester or a wooden toothpick inserted in the center comes out clean. Allow to cool completely in the pans. Run a blunt knife around the rim of each cake to release the edges, invert onto a wire rack, and carefully peel off the paper liners.

6 To assemble the cake, place one layer of cake on a cake stand or serving plate, flat side up. Using a brush, generously moisten the top of the layer with $1/4$ cup of the Grand Marnier Syrup; then spread 1 cup of the Orange–Grand Marnier Frosting evenly over it. Repeat with the second layer and more syrup and frosting. Top off with the third layer, flat side up. Brush with the last of the syrup and frost the top and sides of the cake with the remaining frosting. Garnish with candied orange peel and white chocolate shavings.

$1/4$ cup sugar

$1/2$ cup water

$1/4$ cup Grand Marnier

grand marnier syrup   MAKES 3/4 CUP

Combine the sugar and water in a small saucepan. Bring to a simmer, stirring to dissolve the sugar. Continue to cook, without stirring, until the syrup is reduced to $1/2$ cup. Remove from the heat. Let cool completely, then stir in the Grand Marnier.

6 ounces fine-quality white chocolate, coarsely chopped

2 $1/2$ cups heavy cream

2 tablespoons Grand Marnier

1 tablespoon grated orange zest

orange–grand marnier frosting   MAKES ABOUT 6 CUPS

1 In a medium heatproof bowl, melt the white chocolate with $1/2$ cup of the cream over barely simmering water. Stir until smooth. Remove from the heat and allow to cool to room temperature. Stir in the Grand Marnier and orange zest.

2 In a large chilled bowl with chilled beaters, whip the remaining 2 cups cream until almost completely stiff. Add the whipped cream to the white chocolate mixture and gently fold it in.

piña colada cake

1 can (20 ounces) crushed pineapple in juice (no sugar added)

1 cup sugar

¹/₄ cup freshly squeezed lime juice

1 one-inch piece of vanilla bean, split in half

Brown Sugar Cake (page 118)

Coconut Buttercream (page 119)

²/₃ cup rum (light, amber, or dark, whichever you prefer)

Coconut flakes and thin slices of fresh or dried pineapple, for decoration

All the great flavors of the island cocktail go into this festive cake: pineapple, coconut, lime, and rum. It's a high, light, and handsome cake that can turn any dinner into a party.

MAKES A 9-INCH TRIPLE-LAYER CAKE; SERVES 16 TO 20

1   Combine the crushed pineapple, sugar, and lime juice in a large nonreactive skillet. With the tip of a small knife, scrape the vanilla seeds into the pan; add the pod as well. Warm over medium-low heat, stirring to dissolve the sugar, 2 to 3 minutes.

2   Raise the heat to medium and simmer, stirring occasionally to prevent scorching, until the juices have almost completely evaporated and the pineapple has a jamlike consistency. Remove from the heat and discard the vanilla pod. Let the pineapple filling cool completely before using. (The filling can be made a day ahead and refrigerated. Let return to room temperature before using.)

3   Bake the Brown Sugar Cake as directed. Let the layers cool completely. Prepare the Coconut Buttercream just before you're ready to use it.

4   To assemble the cake, place one layer, flat side up, on a cake stand or serving plate. Sprinkle a generous 3 tablespoons rum over the cake. Spread half of the pineapple filling over the layer, leaving a ¹/₄-inch margin around the edge. Add the second layer, sprinkle with more rum, and cover with the remaining filling. Top with the third layer, flat side up, and sprinkle with the remaining rum. Frost the top and sides of the cake with the Coconut Buttercream. Decorate with some coconut shreds and thin slices of pineapple.

CONTINUED

3 3/4 cups cake flour

1 3/4 teaspoons baking soda

1 teaspoon baking powder

1/2 teaspoon salt

2 1/4 cups packed light brown sugar

2 sticks (8 ounces) unsalted butter,
at room temperature

1 3/4 cups buttermilk

5 eggs

2 teaspoons vanilla extract

brown sugar cake   MAKES THREE 9-INCH LAYERS

1 Preheat the oven to 350 degrees F. Butter three 9-inch cake pans. Line the bottom of each pan with a round of parchment or waxed paper and butter the paper.

2 Sift together the flour, baking soda, baking powder, and salt into a large mixer bowl; whisk gently to combine. Add the brown sugar, butter, and 1 1/2 cups of the buttermilk to the dry ingredients. With the mixer on low, blend to incorporate. Raise the speed to medium and beat until light and fluffy, 2 to 3 minutes.

3 Whisk the eggs with the remaining 1/4 cup buttermilk and the vanilla and add to the batter in 3 additions, scraping down the sides of the bowl well and beating only long enough to incorporate between additions. Divide the batter among the 3 prepared pans.

4 Bake for 25 to 28 minutes, or until a cake tester or wooden toothpick inserted in the center comes out clean. Let the layers cool in the pans for 10 minutes; then turn out onto wire racks, carefully peel off the paper liners, and allow to cool completely before filling and frosting.

3 egg whites

1 cup sugar

¹/₄ cup water

2 ¹/₂ sticks (10 ounces) unsalted butter, at room temperature

²/₃ cup unsweetened coconut milk

1 ¹/₂ teaspoons coconut extract

coconut buttercream   MAKES ABOUT 5 CUPS

1 Put the egg whites in the bowl of an electric mixer fitted with the whip attachment so they are all ready to go.

2 Combine the sugar and water in a small heavy saucepan and place over medium heat, stirring to dissolve the sugar. Bring to a boil and cook, without stirring, until the syrup reaches the soft-ball stage, 238 degrees F on a candy thermometer.

3 Beat the egg whites briefly at medium speed. Slowly add the hot syrup in a thin stream, being careful to avoid the beaters. Continue to whip until the meringue has cooled to body temperature.

4 With the mixer on low speed, gradually add the butter, several tablespoons at a time, and continue to beat until a smooth, fluffy frosting forms.

5 Add the coconut milk in several additions, scraping down the sides of the bowl well after each addition. Add the coconut extract and mix until smooth.

nut and spice cakes

almond-raspberry cake

This gossamer ivory cake is a great choice for a sweet-sixteen party, an anniversary, or even a small wedding. Tart raspberries—both fresh and preserved—offset the intense almond flavor beautifully.

4 ¹/₂ cups cake flour

4 ¹/₂ teaspoons baking powder

³/₄ teaspoon salt

2 ¹/₂ sticks (10 ounces) unsalted butter, at room temperature

2 ²/₃ cups sugar

1 tablespoon almond extract

²/₃ cup prepared almond paste (7 ounces)

10 egg whites

1 ¹/₂ cups whole milk

1 cup seedless raspberry preserves

Almond Buttercream Frosting (facing page)

Fresh raspberries and toasted sliced almonds, for decoration

BAKER'S NOTE

For easiest assembly and frosting, it is best to bake the cake layers a day ahead. Let them cool completely, then wrap well and refrigerate. It is much simpler to ice and decorate cold layers. For best flavor and texture, though, be sure to let the finished cake return to room temperature before serving.

MAKES A 9-INCH TRIPLE-LAYER CAKE; SERVES 16 TO 20

1 Preheat the oven to 350 degrees F. Butter the bottoms and sides of three 9-inch round cake pans. Line the bottom of each pan with a round of parchment or waxed paper and butter the paper.

2 In a medium bowl, sift together the cake flour, baking powder, and salt. Set the dry ingredients aside.

3 In a large mixer bowl, combine the butter, sugar, and almond extract. Break up the almond paste into small pieces and add to the bowl. With an electric mixer on medium-high speed, beat until light and fluffy. Gradually add the egg whites 2 or 3 at a time, beating just long enough to incorporate after each addition. Scrape down the sides of the bowl several times to make sure the batter is evenly mixed.

4 Dust about a third of the dry ingredients over the batter and fold in with a large rubber spatula until just combined. Fold in about half the milk. Fold in half the remaining flour mixture, followed by the remaining milk. Finally, fold in the last of the dry ingredients just until no streaks of white remain. Use a light hand and do not overmix. Divide the batter among the 3 prepared cake pans.

5 Bake for 25 to 30 minutes, or until a cake tester or wooden toothpick stuck into the center comes out clean. Let the cakes cool in their pans on wire racks for about 10 minutes. Turn out onto wire racks, carefully peel off the paper liners, and let the layers cool completely, at least 1 hour.

6 To assemble the cake, place one layer, flat side up, on a cake stand or serving plate. Spread ¹/₂ cup of the raspberry preserves over the cake, leaving a ¹/₄-inch margin around the edges. Repeat with the second layer and remaining preserves. Finally, add the third layer and spread the Almond Buttercream Frosting over the top and sides of the cake. If you have any frosting remaining, use a medium star tip to pipe a border around the top rim. Decorate the top of the cake with fresh raspberries and garnish the bottom edge with toasted almonds, if desired.

1 cup sugar

¹/₄ cup water

3 egg whites

3 sticks (12 ounces) unsalted butter, at room temperature

2 teaspoons almond extract

almond buttercream frosting   MAKES ABOUT 3 ¹/₂ CUPS

1 In a small heavy saucepan, combine the sugar with the water, stirring to dissolve the sugar. Bring to a boil over medium heat, without stirring, washing down the sides of the pan with a wet pastry brush a couple of times to dissolve any sugar crystals, until the syrup reaches the soft-ball stage, 238 degrees F on a candy thermometer.

2 In a large mixer bowl, beat the egg whites with an electric mixer on medium speed until frothy. Continue beating while gradually adding the hot syrup in a slow stream, taking care to avoid hitting the beaters, or the syrup may splatter. When all the syrup has been added, raise the speed to medium-high and continue to whip until the mixture is very fluffy and has cooled to body temperature.

3 Reduce the mixer speed to medium-low and gradually add the butter 2 or 3 tablespoons at a time. As you're adding the last few tablespoons of butter, the mixture will appear to break, then suddenly come together like whipped butter. Beat in the almond extract.

toasted almond tea cake

This is a lovely cake to serve for a garden party or afternoon tea. Tart, fresh Lemon Curd is refreshing and cuts through the sweetness of the rest of the cake.

²/3 cup sliced almonds
(see Baker's Note, page 127)

2 ²/3 cups cake flour

1 ³/4 cups sugar

4 ¹/2 teaspoons baking powder

¹/2 teaspoon salt

1 ¹/3 cups sour cream

2 sticks (8 ounces) unsalted butter,
at room temperature

2 whole eggs

4 egg yolks

1 tablespoon almond extract

¹/2 cup raspberry preserves,
preferably seedless

Lemon Curd (page 126)

Amaretto Glaze (page 127)

MAKES AN 8-INCH TRIPLE-LAYER CAKE; SERVES 12 TO 16

1 Preheat the oven to 350 degrees F. Butter three 8-inch round cake pans. Line the bottom of each pan with a round of parchment or waxed paper and butter the paper. Spread out the almonds on a baking sheet and toast until fragrant and lightly browned, 5 to 7 minutes.

2 Combine ¹/2 cup of the toasted almond slices, the flour, sugar, baking powder, and salt in a large mixer bowl. (Set aside the remaining toasted almond slices for decoration.) With an electric mixer on low speed, blend well. Add the sour cream and butter and blend to incorporate. Raise the speed to medium and beat until light and fluffy, about 2 minutes.

3 Put the whole eggs and egg yolks in a medium bowl and whisk together. Whisk in the almond extract. Add the eggs to the batter in 2 or 3 additions, scraping down the sides of the bowl after each addition and beating only until the eggs are incorporated. Divide among the 3 prepared cake pans.

4 Bake the cake layers for 27 to 30 minutes, or until a cake tester or wooden toothpick inserted in the center comes out clean. Allow to cool in the pans for 10 minutes, then turn out onto a wire rack and gently peel off the paper liners. While the cakes are still warm, spread 2 to 3 tablespoons of the raspberry preserves over the flat side of each layer. Let cool completely.

CONTINUED

5 To assemble the cake, place one layer, raspberry preserve side up, on a cake stand or serving plate. Spread half of the Lemon Curd over the layer, right to the edge. Repeat with the second layer and the remaining Lemon Curd and top off with the final layer of cake. Pour the Amaretto Glaze onto the center of the top layer and gently spread it to the edge, allowing it to slowly drizzle down the sides of the cake decoratively, like icicles. After it has had a few minutes to drip and the glaze has set, sprinkle the remaining toasted sliced almonds over the top.

1/2 cup sugar

1 tablespoon cornstarch

1/2 cup freshly squeezed lemon juice (from 3 or 4 lemons)

4 egg yolks (see Baker's Note, facing page)

2 tablespoons unsalted butter, at room temperature

Grated zest from 1 lemon

lemon curd   MAKES ABOUT 1 CUP

Freshly squeezed lemon juice and grated zest give this a bright citrus flavor. The curd can be made up to a day in advance.

1 Put the sugar and cornstarch in a small nonreactive saucepan and whisk to blend. Add the lemon juice and eggs yolks and whisk until smooth. Bring to a full boil over medium-low heat, whisking constantly. Allow to boil for a full minute, still whisking.

2 Pour through a mesh strainer into a glass dish. Whisk in the butter and lemon zest until blended. Let cool slightly, then cover with plastic wrap, pressing it down onto the surface of the curd to prevent a skin from forming. Refrigerate until cold and set, at least 1 hour. Stir well before using.

2 cups confectioners' sugar

2 tablespoons amaretto liqueur

amaretto glaze   MAKES ABOUT 3/4 CUP

Sift the sugar into a bowl. Add the amaretto and mix. Add about 1 tablespoon water a bit at a time—all may not be needed—to make a thick pasty glaze.

chocolate-hazelnut gianduja cake

Gianduja is an Italian word that's used throughout the baking world to signify the marriage of chocolate and hazelnuts. Here a light hazelnut cake is filled and frosted with a simple gianduja cream, made from flavored chocolate that you can buy almost anywhere fine chocolate is sold, including the imported chocolate section of your supermarket.

½ cup hazelnuts
(see Baker's Note, page 130)

1 ¼ cups sugar

1 ⅓ cups cake flour

1 teaspoon baking powder

½ teaspoon salt

6 eggs, separated

3 tablespoons hazelnut oil,
preferably imported

⅓ cup water

¼ teaspoon cream of tartar

Vanilla Syrup (page 130)
(see Baker's Note, page 130)

Gianduja Frosting (page 131)

MAKES AN 8-INCH TRIPLE-LAYER CAKE; SERVES 12 TO 16

1 Preheat the oven to 350 degrees F. Line the bottoms of three 8-inch round cake pans with rounds of parchment or waxed paper. Do not grease the pans.

2 Spread out the hazelnuts in a small baking pan and toast until fragrant and lightly browned, 7 to 10 minutes. Remove and rub in a kitchen towel to remove as much of the dark outer skins as possible. Let cool. Set aside half the hazelnuts for garnish.

3 Place ¼ cup of the toasted hazelnuts in the bowl of a food processor with 1 cup of the sugar. Pulse just until the nuts are finely ground.

4 Transfer the ground nuts to a large bowl. Sift the flour, baking powder, and salt over the nuts; stir to mix. Using a whisk, blend in the egg yolks, hazelnut oil, and water.

5 Put the egg whites and cream of tartar in a large, clean mixer bowl, and with the mixer on medium, whip until frothy. Slowly add the remaining ¼ cup sugar and beat until soft peaks form. Do not whip until stiff, or the cake will be dry. Add one-fourth of the beaten whites to the batter and gently fold in with a large spatula. Fold in the remaining whites, taking care not to deflate the batter. Divide among the 3 prepared pans.

CONTINUED

6 Bake the cake layers for 18 to 20 minutes, or until a cake tester or wooden toothpick inserted in the center comes out clean. Let the cakes cool completely in the pans on wire racks. When they are cool, run a blunt knife around the edges to release the cake layers, then invert onto a wire rack and peel off the paper liners. (These cakes can be baked a day ahead, wrapped tightly in plastic, and stored at room temperature.)

7 To assemble the cake, place one layer, flat side up, on a cake stand or serving dish. Brush about 3 tablespoons of the Vanilla Syrup over the layer. Spread 1 cup of the Gianduja Frosting over the layer. Repeat with the second layer, with more syrup and another cup of the frosting. Top with the third layer, flat side up. Moisten with the remaining syrup. Cover the top and sides of the cake with the remaining frosting. Use the back of a spoon or an offset palette knife to create swirls all over. Decorate with the reserved whole toasted hazelnuts.

$1/3$ cup sugar

$2/3$ cup water

1 teaspoon vanilla extract

vanilla syrup MAKES $2/3$ CUP

This easy syrup can be made up to a week in advance and refrigerated. Let return to room temperature before using.

1 Combine the sugar and water in a small saucepan. Bring to a simmer over medium heat, stirring to dissolve the sugar. Continue to simmer until the syrup reduces to $2/3$ cup.

2 Remove from the heat and stir in the vanilla. Cool completely before using.

8 ounces gianduja chocolate,
coarsely chopped

2 ¹/₂ cups heavy cream

gianduja frosting   MAKES ABOUT 6 CUPS

Scharffen Berger makes an excellent dark gianduja chocolate that is available in some upscale supermarkets and by mail order (see page 213). Be sure to use this ganache soon after it is made, before the chocolate sets.

1 In a double boiler or a medium heatproof bowl over simmering water, heat the chocolate and ¹/₂ cup of the cream until the chocolate melts. Remove from the heat and stir until smooth. Transfer to a large bowl and let cool to room temperature but do not allow the chocolate to set.

2 In a chilled bowl with chilled beaters, whip the remaining 2 cups cream until almost stiff. Fold the whipped cream into the chocolate just until no white streaks remain.

ginger chiffon cake with key lime curd and lime buttercream

○○○

Two kinds of lime in the filling and frosting provide a tart counterpoint to the fresh bite of ginger in this light, summery cake. Enjoy it with a cool glass of iced tea.

6 eggs, separated

1/4 cup neutral vegetable oil, such as canola, soybean, or vegetable blend

2 tablespoons grated fresh ginger

6 tablespoons water

1 1/2 cups sugar

1 1/3 cups cake flour

1 teaspoon baking powder

1/2 teaspoon salt

1/2 teaspoon cream of tartar

Key Lime Curd (page 134)

Lime Buttercream (page 135)

Fresh mint sprigs or lime leaves, for decoration

MAKES AN 8-INCH TRIPLE-LAYER CAKE; SERVES 12 TO 16

1 Preheat the oven to 350 degrees F. Line the bottoms of three 8-inch round cake pans with parchment or waxed paper; do not grease.

2 In a medium mixing bowl, whisk together the egg yolks, oil, ginger, and water; set aside.

3 Sift 1 cup of the sugar, the flour, baking powder, and salt into a large mixing bowl; whisk gently to combine. Add the egg yolk mixture and whisk to form a smooth batter.

4 Place the egg whites in a large mixer bowl and beat with an electric mixer fitted with the whip attachment on medium-high speed until frothy. Slowly add the remaining 1/2 cup sugar and the cream of tartar and continue to whip until soft, droopy peaks form. Fold one-fourth of the beaten egg whites into the batter, taking care not to deflate the mixture. Gently fold in the remaining whites. Divide the batter among the 3 prepared pans.

5 Bake for about 18 minutes, or until a cake tester or wooden toothpick inserted in the center comes out clean. Allow the layers to cool completely in the pans. To remove, run a blunt knife around the edges, invert each pan, and tap out the cake onto a wire rack. Peel off the paper.

6 While the cakes are baking and cooling, make the Key Lime Curd and chill completely.

CONTINUED

7 To assemble the cake, place one cake layer on a cake stand or serving plate and spread half of the Key Lime Curd over the top, leaving a generous $1/4$-inch margin around the edges. Repeat with another cake layer and the remaining lime curd. Top with the third layer. Frost all over with the Lime Buttercream. Decorate with fresh mint sprigs or lime leaves.

6 egg yolks

1 tablespoon cornstarch

6 tablespoons sugar

6 tablespoons Key lime juice (see Baker's Note, facing page)

2 tablespoons unsalted butter, at room temperature

key lime curd   MAKES ABOUT 1 1/4 CUPS

1 In a medium bowl, whisk together the egg yolks and cornstarch. Combine the sugar and lime juice in a non-reactive saucepan and whisk in the egg yolks. Bring to a boil over medium-low heat, whisking gently the entire time. Allow to boil for 1 minute.

2 Pour through a mesh strainer into a heatproof bowl and whisk in the butter until it is completely melted. Let cool slightly, then cover with plastic wrap, pressing it directly onto the surface to prevent a skin from forming. Refrigerate until cold, at least 1 hour.

4 egg whites

1 cup sugar

1/3 cup freshly squeezed lime juice

3 sticks (12 ounces) unsalted butter, at room temperature

BAKER'S NOTE

Key limes are tiny pale green limes that are mildly acidic. Occasionally they appear fresh in the market, often bundled in mesh bags; you can squeeze these just like lemons. Bottled Key lime juice is available year-round and is much more convenient. It works just as well in this recipe.

lime buttercream   MAKES ABOUT 4 CUPS

This is a lighter buttercream that uses only the whites of the eggs to make an Italian meringue—that is, a meringue made with a syrup.

1 Place the egg whites in a large mixing bowl and set the mixer up with the whip attachment.

2 In a nonreactive saucepan, heat the sugar and lime juice, stirring to dissolve the sugar. Bring to a boil and cook, without stirring, until the syrup reaches the soft-ball stage, 238 degrees F on a candy thermometer.

3 Turn the mixer to medium-low speed and slowly add the syrup to the egg whites, taking care not to pour it onto the beaters. Beat on medium speed until the meringue cools to body temperature.

4 With the mixer on medium-low, gradually add the butter several tablespoons at a time. Beat until a smooth buttery frosting forms.

gingerbread beer cake with bittersweet chocolate frosting

2 ¹/₄ cups cake flour

2 cups sugar

4 teaspoons unsweetened cocoa powder

4 ¹/₂ teaspoons ground ginger

1 tablespoon ground cinnamon

1 ¹/₂ teaspoons grated nutmeg

1 ¹/₂ teaspoons powdered mustard

³/₄ teaspoon ground cloves

¹/₂ teaspoon ground cardamom

2 ¹/₄ teaspoons baking powder

¹/₂ teaspoon baking soda

¹/₂ teaspoon salt

³/₄ cup dark beer or porter
(see Baker's Note)

¹/₂ cup unsulphured molasses

6 tablespoons buttermilk

1 ¹/₂ teaspoons vanilla extract

1 ¹/₂ sticks (6 ounces) unsalted butter,
at room temperature

3 eggs

Bittersweet Chocolate Frosting
(facing page)

Mustard and beer—sounds more like a pub sandwich than a cake. But dessert it is! Actually, you don't taste the powdered mustard; it merely contributes a bit of heat on the tongue, which is appropriate for gingerbread. And the dark beer adds richness and deepens the flavor. If you like gingerbread, you'll love this cake.

MAKES AN 8-INCH TRIPLE-LAYER CAKE; SERVES 12 TO 16

1 Preheat the oven to 350 degrees F. Butter three 8-inch round cake pans. Line the bottom of each pan with a round of parchment or waxed paper and butter the paper.

2 Measure the flour, sugar, cocoa powder, ginger, cinnamon, nutmeg, mustard, cloves, cardamom, baking powder, baking soda, and salt into a large mixer bowl. With an electric mixer on low speed, blend the dry ingredients well, about 30 seconds.

3 In a medium bowl, combine the beer, molasses, buttermilk, and vanilla; whisk well to combine. Add the softened butter and two-thirds of the beer mixture to the spiced flour and beat with the mixer on low speed until well blended. Raise the speed to medium and beat well to aerate, about 3 minutes, or until the mixture is lighter and somewhat fluffy.

4 Add the eggs to the remaining beer mixture and whisk to blend well. Add this liquid to the batter in 2 or 3 additions, beating on medium speed and scraping down the bowl several times. Divide the batter among the 3 prepared pans.

5 Bake for 25 to 30 minutes, or until a cake tester or wooden toothpick inserted in the center comes out clean. Let the layers cool in their pans for 10 minutes. Then turn out onto wire racks, carefully peel off the paper liners, and let cool completely, at least 1 hour.

6 To frost the cake, place one layer, flat side up, on a cake stand or serving plate. Top with $^2/_3$ cup of the Bittersweet Chocolate Frosting. Spread evenly over the layer right to the edge; repeat with the second layer. Add the final layer and frost the top and sides with the remaining frosting.

7 To decorate the cake, use an offset spatula or the back of a spoon to swirl the frosting on the top and sides. Then, touch the frosting gently with the spatula and quickly pull it up to create a spike. Repeat all over the cake. Let set at room temperature for at least 30 minutes before cutting, so the frosting has a chance to set up.

bittersweet chocolate frosting MAKES ABOUT 4 1/2 CUPS

1 Melt the chocolate with the cream in a double boiler or a metal bowl set over a pan of simmering water. Whisk to blend well. Remove from the heat and let stand, whisking occasionally, until the chocolate cream sets up, or thickens, to the consistency of mayonnaise.

2 Place the butter in a large mixer bowl and with an electric mixer on medium speed, whip the butter until light and fluffy. Add the chocolate cream and whip until lighter in color and somewhat stiff, about 3 minutes. Do not whip too long, or the frosting may begin to separate.

BAKER'S NOTE

The choice of beer here is important. A light lager beer will be too bitter. Stout is too heavy. A good dark beer will contribute a slightly chocolaty sweetness and depth of flavor that is extremely pleasing with the spices. A Samuel Smith Taddy Porter, an English brew, was the final choice when testing.

10 ounces bittersweet chocolate (60 to 65 percent cocoa is ideal)

1 1/2 cups heavy cream

1 1/2 sticks (6 ounces) unsalted butter, at room temperature

pistachio petit four cake

Marzipan, apricot preserves, and a dark chocolate glaze turn a pistachio butter cake into an irresistible dessert reminiscent of European *petits fours glacés.*

3/4 cup skinned pistachio nuts

1 2/3 cups sugar

2 cups cake flour

1 tablespoon baking powder

1/2 teaspoon salt

2 sticks (8 ounces) unsalted butter, at room temperature

1/2 cup milk

2 teaspoons vanilla extract

5 eggs, lightly beaten

Marzipan (page 141); marzipan roses for decoration (optional; see box on page 141)

3/4 cup apricot preserves

Dark Ganache Glaze (page 140)

MAKES AN 8-INCH TRIPLE-LAYER CAKE; SERVES 12 TO 16

1 Preheat the oven to 350 degrees F. Butter three 8-inch round cake pans. Line the bottom of each pan with a round of parchment or waxed paper and butter the paper.

2 Spread out the pistachios in a baking pan and toast in the oven for 7 to 10 minutes, or until lightly colored. Transfer to a dish and let cool completely. Finely chop the pistachios and set 1/4 cup aside for decoration.

3 Put the remaining 1/2 cup pistachios in a food processor. Add the sugar and pulse just enough to grind them finely. Pour into a large mixing bowl and add the flour, baking powder, and salt. Blend with the mixer on low for 30 seconds.

4 Add the butter, milk, and vanilla and, with the mixer on low, beat until completely incorporated. Raise the speed to medium and beat until light and fluffy, 2 to 3 minutes. Add the beaten eggs in 2 or 3 additions, scraping down the sides of the bowl well and mixing only long enough to blend after each addition. Divide the batter among the 3 prepared pans.

5 Bake for about 25 minutes, or until a cake tester or wooden toothpick inserted in the center comes out clean. Allow the layers to cool in the pans for 10 minutes. Turn out onto wire racks, carefully peel off the paper liners, and let cool completely.

CONTINUED

6 Roll out a third of the Marzipan on a work surface dusted with a little confectioners' sugar to about $1/8$-inch thickness. Set one of the cake pans upside down on the Marzipan and trim around it with a small knife to make an 8-inch round. Repeat two more times with the remaining Marzipan. Save all your scraps to make roses for decoration, if you like.

7 To assemble the cake, place one cake layer on a cake board, flat side up. Spread $1/4$ cup of the preserves evenly over the top, leaving a $1/4$-inch margin all around. Place one Marzipan round on top of the preserves and spread $1/3$ cup of the Dark Ganache Glaze over the Marzipan so that it completely covers the surface. Repeat with the second layer, adding more preserves, another round of Marzipan, and more Dark Ganache Glaze. Top the cake with the third layer. Spread the last of the apricot preserves over the top of the cake and cover it with the last round of Marzipan.

8 Place the cake on a wire cooling rack that is nesting in a baking pan. Pour the remaining Dark Ganache Glaze over the cake, in several additions, spreading to coat the top and sides. Allow the ganache to set. Garnish the cake with the reserved chopped toasted pistachio nuts and a single marzipan rose or several smaller roses.

1 pound extra-bittersweet chocolate

1 $1/4$ cups heavy cream

dark ganache glaze MAKES ABOUT 3 CUPS

Chop the chocolate coarsely and put it in a heatproof bowl. Bring the cream to a bare simmer. Pour the hot cream over the chocolate and let stand for 5 minutes. Whisk until smooth and use the glaze soon after making so that it doesn't set.

8 ounces almond paste

1 1/2 cups confectioners' sugar

1/4 cup light corn syrup

MAKING MARZIPAN ROSES

1 First tint the marzipan, if desired, by kneading in a tiny amount of paste food coloring, dabbing just a small bit onto the marzipan with the tip of a tooth-pick. (Unlike ordinary food coloring, paste colors are highly concentrated.)

2 Flatten the tinted marzipan into a disk and roll out on a work surface dusted with confectioners' sugar or between 2 sheets of waxed paper to a sheet 1/8 inch thick.

3 With a 1 1/2-inch round cookie cutter, cut out 8 or 9 circles. Cover all the marzipan you are not using immediately with plastic wrap so it doesn't dry out.

4 Roll one piece of marzipan into a ball the size of a marble and pinch with your fingers to shape into a cone about 1 to 1 1/4 inches high, tapering to a fine point at the top.

5 Take another round of marzipan and wrap it like a petal around the cone, pinching it at the bottom to adhere and at the top to thin and ruffle slightly like a flower. Repeat with the remaining "petals," overlapping slightly as you work your way around. If necessary, use a little water to help glue the marzipan in place.

marzipan MAKES ABOUT 10 OUNCES

Crumble the almond paste into a large mixing bowl. Use an electric mixer on low speed to soften the almond paste. Add the confectioners' sugar and corn syrup and beat until smooth. Wrap well in plastic so it doesn't dry out, and allow to rest at room temperature for 1 to 2 hours before rolling out.

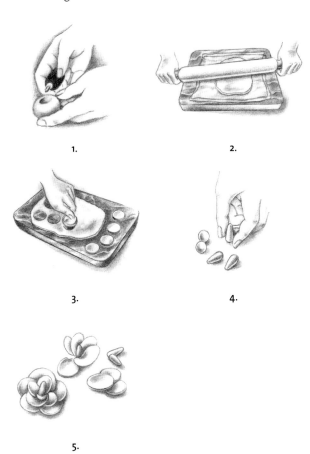

1.

2.

3.

4.

5.

maple-walnut cake

There's a reason maple and walnut are often married as a single flavor: the two are exceptionally compatible and have an almost synergistic effect on each other. Here maple syrup is used both to sweeten and flavor the cake as well as the frosting.

1 1/3 cups walnut halves
(see Baker's Note, page 144)

3 cups cake flour

1 1/4 cups packed light brown sugar

2 1/4 teaspoons ground cinnamon

1 3/4 teaspoons baking soda

3/4 teaspoon salt

1 1/2 sticks (6 ounces) unsalted butter,
at room temperature

1 1/2 cups pure maple syrup, preferably
light amber (see Baker's Note, page 144)

1 whole egg

1 egg yolk

1 cup milk

Maple Cream Frosting (page 144)

MAKES AN 8-INCH TRIPLE-LAYER CAKE; SERVES 12 TO 16

1 Preheat the oven to 350 degrees F. Butter three 8-inch round cake pans. Line the bottom of each with a round of parchment or waxed paper and butter the paper.

2 Spread out the walnuts on a small baking sheet and toast in the oven until fragrant and lightly toasted, 7 to 10 minutes. Transfer to a dish and let cool. Leave the oven on. When the nuts are cool, set aside 1/3 cup for garnish. Finely chop the remaining toasted walnuts.

3 Combine the chopped walnuts, flour, brown sugar, cinnamon, baking soda, and salt in a large mixer bowl. With the mixer on low, blend well. Add the butter and maple syrup and beat until blended. Raise the speed to medium and beat until light and fluffy, about 2 minutes.

4 In a medium bowl, whisk together the whole egg, egg yolk, and milk. Add this liquid to the batter in 2 or 3 additions, beating until blended and scraping down the sides of the bowl well after each addition. Divide the batter among the 3 prepared pans.

5 Bake for 32 to 35 minutes, or until a cake tester or wooden toothpick inserted in the center comes out clean. Let the cakes cool in the pans for 10 minutes, then turn out onto wire racks, gently peel off the paper liners, and let cool completely.

CONTINUED

6 To assemble the cake, place one cake layer, flat side up, on a cake stand or serving plate. Spread $2/3$ cup frosting over the layer, spreading it evenly right to the edge. Repeat with the second layer and another $2/3$ cup frosting. Set the third layer on top and frost the top and sides with the remaining frosting, swirling the frosting decoratively with an offset palette knife or the back of a spoon. Garnish with the reserved toasted walnut halves.

2 sticks (8 ounces) unsalted butter, at room temperature

$2/3$ cup maple syrup

12 ounces cream cheese, at room temperature

6 cups confectioners' sugar, sifted after measuring

BAKER'S NOTES

o Be sure your walnuts are impeccably fresh. It will make all the difference in the world here.

o When purchasing pure maple syrup, it's helpful to know a few things: Vermont labels their best syrup as "grade A," while other states that make excellent syrup, such as Pennsylvania, do not. Instead, they use an intensity rating—light amber, which would correspond with Grade A; medium amber; and dark amber. These grada-tions can vary from producer to producer, so it's wise to taste if you can. Many people find that dark amber syrup has more flavor than the lighter syrups, and it certainly can be used here.

maple cream frosting   MAKES ABOUT 4 CUPS

1 Place the butter in a wide medium saucepan and melt over low heat. Add the maple syrup, raise the heat to medium-low, and boil for 5 minutes, stirring frequently so the syrup does not burn.

2 Pour the hot maple butter into a heatproof bowl and let cool to room temperature.

3 Place the cream cheese in a large mixing bowl and beat well with an electric mixer to lighten. Gradually add the confectioners' sugar and beat until smooth. Scrape down the bowl well and continue to beat until light and fluffy. Add the maple butter and mix until completely blended.

scotch whisky cake

Studded with raisins and walnuts, filled with bitter orange marmalade that balances the sweetness of the cake, and covered with a razor-tart lemon icing, this is a cake for grown-up tastes. For a distinctive flavor, be sure to use a good, smoky Scotch.

1 ½ cups walnut pieces

2 cups dark raisins, or a mix of dark and golden

3 cups all-purpose flour

2 ½ teaspoons baking soda

1 teaspoon ground mace

⅓ cup Scotch whisky

3 tablespoons freshly squeezed lemon juice

2 sticks (8 ounces) unsalted butter, at room temperature

1 ½ cups packed light brown sugar

3 eggs

1 ½ cups orange marmalade

Tart Lemon Icing (page 146)

MAKES AN 8-INCH TRIPLE-LAYER CAKE; SERVES 12 TO 16

1 Preheat the oven to 350 degrees F. Butter three 8-inch round cake pans. Line the bottoms with rounds of parchment or waxed paper and butter the paper.

2 Toast the walnuts on a baking sheet for 7 to 10 minutes. Allow them to cool and chop them into small pieces with a large knife or by pulsing in a food processor. (If you use a processor, be careful not to grind the nuts to a paste.)

3 While the nuts are toasting, with a large sharp knife, coarsely chop the raisins. Place them in a small saucepan and add just enough water to barely cover them. Bring to a boil, remove from the heat, and let stand until plumped. Drain the raisins, reserving ⅓ cup of the liquid; let cool completely.

4 Sift the flour, baking soda, and mace into a medium bowl and set aside. In a small bowl, combine the Scotch, lemon juice, and reserved raisin liquid.

5 In a large mixer bowl, cream the butter with the brown sugar until light and fluffy. Add the eggs one at a time, scraping down the bowl well between additions and beating only enough to incorporate the eggs. Add the dry ingredients and liquid alternately to the batter in 2 or 3 additions, scraping down the bowl after each addition. Be careful not to overmix. Divide the batter among the 3 prepared pans.

CONTINUED

6 Bake for 25 to 28 minutes, or until a cake tester or a wooden toothpick inserted in the center comes out clean. Let cool in the pans for 10 minutes, then invert onto cooling racks and carefully peel off the paper liners. Let cool completely, at least 1 hour.

7 To assemble the cake, put one layer, flat side up, on a cake stand or serving plate. Spread about $1/2$ cup of the orange marmalade evenly over the cake, leaving a $1/4$-inch margin around the edges. Repeat this with the second layer. Top with the third layer and spread the marmalade to the very edge of the layer. Finally, ice the sides of the cake with a thin coating of Tart Lemon Icing. With a pastry bag fitted with a small plain tip, pipe a lattice of icing over the marmalade on the top.

2 $1/2$ cups sifted confectioners' sugar

4 tablespoons unsalted butter, at room temperature

2 teaspoons grated lemon zest

$1/3$ cup fresh lemon juice

tart lemon icing   MAKES ABOUT 1 $1/2$ CUPS

In a large bowl, combine the confectioners' sugar, butter, and lemon zest. Blend well with a wooden spoon. Gradually beat in the lemon juice until the icing has a nice, spreading consistency. Add a little extra lemon juice if the frosting is too stiff to spread easily, then beat until smooth and fluffy.

cakes with a world of flavor

cappuccino chiffon cake

To achieve the best flavor here, use freshly brewed espresso, not the powder, which is bitter. To simulate cappuccino, the cake is swathed in whipped cream and topped with a dusting of cocoa or cinnamon, just like the drink.

1/4 cup neutral vegetable oil, such as soybean, canola, or vegetable blend

6 eggs, separated

6 tablespoons freshly brewed espresso, cooled to room temperature

2 teaspoons vanilla extract

1 1/3 cups cake flour

1 1/2 cups sugar

1 teaspoon baking powder

1/2 teaspoon ground cinnamon

1/2 teaspoon salt

1/2 teaspoon cream of tartar

Espresso Syrup (facing page)

Vanilla Whipped Cream (facing page)

Cocoa powder or ground cinnamon, for dusting

MAKES AN 8-INCH TRIPLE-LAYER CAKE; SERVES 12 TO 16

1 Preheat the oven to 350 degrees F. Line the bottoms of three 8-inch round cake pans with rounds of parchment or waxed paper but do not grease.

2 In a medium bowl, combine the oil, egg yolks, espresso, and vanilla; whisk lightly to blend. In a large mixing bowl, sift together the flour, 1 cup of the sugar, the baking powder, cinnamon, and salt; set the dry ingredients aside.

3 In a large mixer bowl with an electric mixer, whip the egg whites with the cream of tartar on medium-low speed until frothy. Raise the mixer speed to medium-high and gradually add the remaining 1/2 cup sugar. Continue to beat until soft peaks form; do not whip until stiff or the cake will shrink excessively upon cooling.

4 Add the espresso–egg yolk mixture to the dry ingredients and fold together just enough to combine. Add one-fourth of the beaten egg whites and fold them in to lighten the batter. Fold in the remainder of the whites just until no streaks remain. Divide the batter among the 3 prepared pans.

5 Bake the cakes for about 18 minutes, or until a cake tester or wooden toothpick inserted in the center comes out clean. Allow to cool completely in the pans. When cooled, run a blunt knife around the edge of the pans to release the cakes. Invert onto wire racks and remove the paper liners.

6 To assemble the cake, place one layer, flat side up, on a cake stand or serving plate. Soak the cake with $^1/_3$ cup of the Espresso Syrup. Spread about 1 $^1/_3$ cups of the whipped cream evenly over the top of the layer. Repeat with the next layer and more syrup and whipped cream. Finally, top with the third layer. Soak it with the remaining syrup and frost the top and sides with the remaining whipped cream.

7 To decorate the cake, smooth out the cream as much as possible on top with an offset spatula. Lay a paper lace doily over the top of the cake and sift cocoa or cinnamon over the doily. Carefully lift off the doily to reveal the lacy stencil on top of the cake.

$^1/_3$ cup hot, freshly brewed espresso

$^1/_3$ cup sugar

$^1/_3$ cup dark rum, such as Myers's

espresso syrup   MAKES ABOUT 1 CUP

In a bowl, stir together the espresso and sugar until the sugar dissolves. Add the rum and let cool to room temperature.

3 cups heavy cream

$^1/_3$ cup sugar

2 teaspoons vanilla extract

vanilla whipped cream   MAKES ABOUT 6 CUPS

Put the cream, sugar, and vanilla in a large chilled mixing bowl with chilled beaters. With the whip attachment, whip the cream until stiff peaks form.

chai cake with honey-ginger cream

Chai is an Indian spiced black tea served with steamed milk. It's usually sweetened with honey; hence the filling and frosting for this delicately flavored cake.

1 1/3 cups milk

6 chai tea bags without added sweetener, such as Tazo

4 whole eggs

2 egg yolks

2 teaspoons vanilla extract

2 3/4 cups cake flour

2 cups sugar

4 1/2 teaspoons baking powder

3/4 teaspoon ground cinnamon

1/2 teaspoon ground cardamom

1/2 teaspoon salt

2 sticks (8 ounces) unsalted butter, at room temperature

Honey-Ginger Cream (facing page)

MAKES AN 8-INCH TRIPLE-LAYER CAKE; SERVES 12 TO 16

1 Preheat the oven to 350 degrees F. Butter the bottoms and sides of three 8-inch round cake pans. Line the bottoms with rounds of parchment or waxed paper and butter the paper.

2 In a small saucepan, bring the milk to a simmer over medium-low heat. Add the tea bags, being careful not to let the paper tags dip into the milk. Remove from the heat and allow the tea to steep for about 5 minutes. Remove the tea bags, carefully squeezing the milk from them back into the pan. Let the chai milk cool completely.

3 In a medium bowl, combine the whole eggs, egg yolks, vanilla, and 1/3 cup of the chai milk. Whisk to blend.

4 Combine the flour, sugar, baking powder, cinnamon, cardamom, and salt in a large mixer bowl. Beat on low speed for about 30 seconds to blend the dry ingredients. Add the butter and the remaining chai milk and, with the mixer on medium-low, beat to blend well. Raise the speed to medium and beat until light and fluffy. Add the egg mixture in 3 additions, scraping down the sides of the bowl and mixing only to incorporate after each addition. Divide the batter evenly among the 3 prepared pans.

5 Bake the cakes for 26 to 28 minutes, or until a cake tester or wooden toothpick inserted in the center comes out clean. Allow the layers to cool in the pans for about 10 minutes, then turn out onto wire racks. Peel off the paper and let cool completely.

6 To assemble the cake, place one layer, flat side up, on a cake stand or serving plate. Top with $2/3$ cup of the Honey-Ginger Cream. Spread to the edge. Repeat with the next layer. Finally, top with the third cake layer and the remaining Honey-Ginger Cream. Spread this all the way to the edge, allowing small portions to drizzle down the sides like icicles.

2 $1/2$ cups confectioners' sugar

6 ounces cream cheese,
at room temperature

6 tablespoons unsalted butter,
at room temperature

$1/2$ cup honey (any kind,
as long as it is liquid)

$1/2$ teaspoon grated fresh ginger

honey-ginger cream   MAKES ABOUT 2 $1/2$ CUPS

Place all of the ingredients in a food processor. Pulse to incorporate, then scrape down the bowl and process until smooth and well blended.

dulce de leche cake

Translated from the Spanish, *dulce de leche* literally means "milk sweet," and it is, in fact, a caramel made by slowly cooking milk down until it is thick, naturally sweet, and a rich nut brown. Wildly popular throughout Latin America, it has recently taken this country by storm—as a filling, spread, and flavor in cakes, pastries, and ice creams.

8 eggs

1 ⅓ cups packed light brown sugar

1 ⅔ cups cake flour

1 teaspoon ground cinnamon

3 tablespoons unsalted butter, melted and cooled to lukewarm

Rum Syrup (page 156)

Dulce de Leche Cream (page 156)

MAKES AN 8-INCH TRIPLE-LAYER CAKE; SERVES 12 TO 16

1 Preheat the oven to 350 degrees F. Line the bottoms of three 8-inch round cake pans with rounds of parchment or waxed paper but do not grease the pans.

2 In a large heatproof bowl, beat the eggs lightly. Gradually whisk in the brown sugar. Set over a pot of barely simmering water and whisk constantly until the brown sugar dissolves and the mixture warms to body temperature. Remove from the heat and with an electric mixer, beat on medium speed until the mixture holds slowly dissolving ribbons when the beaters are lifted.

3 Put the flour and cinnamon in a sifter and sift about one-third over the top of the eggs. Gently fold in. Repeat 2 more times with the remaining flour, folding only until mixed with no trace of flour.

4 Drizzle the melted butter over the batter and fold in, taking care not to deflate the batter or to leave pockets of butter not folded in. Divide the batter among the 3 prepared cake pans.

CONTINUED

5 Bake for about 15 minutes, or until a cake tester or wooden toothpick inserted in the center comes out clean. Let cool completely in the pans. Run a blunt knife around the edge of each cake to release it from the pan. Turn out onto a wire rack and carefully peel off the paper.

6 To assemble cake, place one cake layer, flat side up, on a cake stand or serving plate. Brush one-third of the Rum Syrup over the cake to moisten evenly. Cover the layer with a bit more than 1 cup of the Dulce de Leche Cream, spreading it evenly to the edges. Repeat with the next layer. Top with the third layer. Moisten it with the remaining syrup. Frost the top and sides of the cake completely with the remaining Dulce de Leche Cream. Then, using a cake comb or the cutting edge of a serrated knife, run it around the side of the cake to make a grooved pattern all around.

$^1/_4$ cup sugar

$^1/_2$ cup water

$^1/_4$ cup rum

rum syrup   MAKES ABOUT $^3/_4$ CUP

Boil the sugar and water over medium heat until the mixture reduces to $^1/_2$ cup. Add the rum off the heat and allow to cool before using.

1 $^1/_3$ cups whole milk (see Baker's Note)

$^1/_2$ cup sugar

$^1/_3$ cup light corn syrup

1 small cinnamon stick

1 one-inch piece of vanilla bean, split lengthwise

3 cups heavy cream

dulce de leche cream   MAKES 6 CUPS

This recipe teaches you how to make dulce de leche, *a rich milk caramel, at home.*

1 Place the milk, sugar, corn syrup, and cinnamon stick in a heavy medium-size saucepan. With the tip of a small knife, scrape the tiny seeds from the inside of the vanilla bean into the pot; toss in the pod as well. Bring to a simmer over medium-low heat, stirring to dissolve the sugar. Continue to simmer, stirring occasionally and scraping the bottom of the pan with a wooden or silicone spatula, until the liquid turns a light amber color, about 45 minutes.

2 Reduce the heat to low and cook, stirring more frequently as the milk darkens and the mixture reduces and thickens, until the color reaches a rich milk caramel (medium brown), 45 to 60 minutes. Watch carefully and stir often near the end, because the milk caramel can burn quickly.

3 Remove and discard the cinnamon stick and vanilla pod and pour the caramel into a heatproof bowl. Let the *dulce de leche* cool slightly, then cover with plastic wrap pressed directly onto the surface to prevent a skin from forming and let cool completely.

4 In a large chilled mixer bowl with chilled beaters, combine the cream with the *dulce de leche*. Beat on low speed to combine and dissolve the *dulce de leche*. Raise the mixer to medium-high and whip until stiff peaks form.

lemon–poppy seed cake with almond–cream cheese frosting

This is an easy cake that is rich and light at the same time, and is best enjoyed freshly baked. The flavor combination of lemon and almond is irresistible. Because the batter contains no egg yolks, it is a very white cake.

3 cups cake flour

2 cups sugar

4 1/2 teaspoons baking powder

1/2 teaspoon salt

3 tablespoons poppy seeds

2 sticks (8 ounces) unsalted butter, at room temperature

Grated zest and juice of 1 large lemon

1 1/4 cups buttermilk

5 egg whites

1/3 cup water

Almond–Cream Cheese Frosting (facing page)

Poppy seeds or sliced almonds, for garnish

MAKES AN 8-INCH TRIPLE-LAYER CAKE; SERVES 12 TO 16

1 Preheat the oven to 350 degrees F. Butter the bottoms of three 8-inch round cake pans. Line the bottom of each pan with a round of parchment or waxed paper; butter the paper.

2 Combine the flour, 1 3/4 cups of the sugar, the baking powder, salt, and poppy seeds in a large mixing bowl. Using an electric mixer on low speed, blend to combine and break up any lumps, about 30 seconds.

3 Add the butter, lemon zest, and 1 cup of the buttermilk to the flour. Beat on low until completely mixed. Raise the speed to medium and beat for 1 to 2 minutes to lighten and aerate the batter.

4 In a medium bowl, combine the egg whites with the remaining 1/4 cup buttermilk; whisk to blend thoroughly. Add the egg white mixture to the batter in 2 or 3 additions, scraping down the sides of the bowl and beating only enough to incorporate. Divide the batter among the 3 prepared pans.

5 Bake for 25 to 30 minutes, or until a cake tester or wooden toothpick inserted in the center comes out clean. Let the cakes cool in the pans for 10 minutes.

6 While the cake layers are cooling, make a lemon syrup. In a small nonreactive saucepan, combine the remaining $1/4$ cup sugar and the lemon juice with the water. Bring to a boil, stirring to dissolve the sugar.

7 Turn out the cake layers onto wire racks and generously brush the hot lemon syrup over the warm cake layers to moisten evenly. Allow the layers to cool completely.

8 To frost the cake, place one layer, flat side up, on a cake stand or serving plate. Spread $2/3$ cup of the Almond–Cream Cheese Frosting over the cake to cover evenly. Repeat with the next layer. Set the third layer in place. Frost the top and sides of the cake with the remaining frosting. Garnish with poppy seeds or sliced almonds.

8 ounces cream cheese, at room temperature

2 sticks (8 ounces) unsalted butter, at room temperature

5 cups confectioners' sugar, sifted

1 tablespoon almond extract

almond–cream cheese frosting MAKES ABOUT 4 1/2 CUPS

In a large mixer bowl, beat the cream cheese and butter with an electric mixer until light and fluffy. Gradually add the confectioners' sugar, 1 cup at a time, beating well after each addition and scraping down the sides of the bowl. Continue to beat until very fluffy, 3 to 4 minutes. Add the almond extract and mix well.

neapolitan rum cake

Here's an adult dessert that's especially nice after a rich Italian meal. The ricotta cheese in the filling must be drained overnight. Since the layers can be baked in advance and the entire dessert tastes better if left to stand for a few hours, or even a day, so the flavors can meld, this is an excellent recipe for entertaining.

8 ounces whole-milk ricotta cheese (see Baker's Note)

Semolina Sponge Cake (page 162)

2 cups heavy cream

$^1/_4$ cup plus 3 tablespoons sugar

1 teaspoon vanilla extract

$^1/_3$ cup chopped dried tart cherries

1 teaspoon grated orange zest

1 tablespoon freshly squeezed orange juice

$^3/_4$ cup light rum

$^1/_4$ cup toasted pine nuts

MAKES AN 8-INCH TRIPLE-LAYER CAKE; SERVES 16 TO 20

1 Line a mesh strainer with a large paper coffee filter or several thicknesses of cheesecloth. Place the ricotta cheese in the filter and set the strainer over a bowl. Cover with plastic wrap and leave in the refrigerator overnight to drain.

2 The next day, bake the cake as directed.

3 While the cake is cooling, make the filling. In a large chilled bowl with chilled beaters, whip the cream until soft peaks form. Gradually beat in $^1/_4$ cup of the sugar and the vanilla and beat until stiff. Set the sweetened whipped cream aside.

4 Put the ricotta in another bowl. Add the remaining 3 tablespoons sugar, the cherries, orange zest, and orange juice. Blend well. Add 1 cup of the sweetened whipped cream and fold in gently.

5 To assemble the cake, place one layer, flat side up, on a cake stand or serving plate. Brush with $^1/_4$ cup of the rum to moisten. Spread half of the ricotta filling evenly over the layer. Repeat with the second layer. Place the third layer of cake on top. Soak this layer with the last of the rum and then frost the top and sides with the remaining whipped cream. Decorate with toasted pine nuts around the top edge of the cake. Refrigerate for at least 3 hours and up to a day before serving.

CONTINUED

BAKER'S NOTE

Be sure to choose a ricotta that does not contain added gums, gelatin, starch, or other stabilizers. You just have to read the label. These additives prevent the cheese from separating from the whey.

8 eggs

1 1/3 cups sugar

2 teaspoons grated orange zest

3 tablespoons semolina flour

1 1/4 cups cake flour

semolina sponge cake MAKES THREE 8-INCH LAYERS

While only a few tablespoons of semolina flour go into the batter, they have a dramatic effect, resulting in a sponge cake with a pleasingly sandy texture.

1 Preheat the oven to 350 degrees F. Line the bottoms of three 8-inch round cake pans with rounds of parchment or waxed paper, but do not grease the pans.

2 Put the eggs and sugar in a large heatproof bowl and whisk lightly to combine. Set over a pot of barely simmering water, taking care not to let the bowl come in contact with the water. Whisk gently and continuously until the sugar dissolves and the mixture is lukewarm to the touch (about 100 degrees F on an instant-read thermometer).

3 Remove from the water bath, add the orange zest, and with an electric mixer fitted with the whip attachment, beat on medium speed until the mixture cools and a slowly dissolving ribbon forms when the beaters are lifted, 7 to 10 minutes.

4 Sift the semolina and cake flours together and return to the sifter. Dust one-third of these dry ingredients over the egg mixture. Gently fold in, deflating the batter as little as possible. Repeat 2 more times until all the dry ingredients are incorporated and no white streaks remain; do not over-mix. Divide the batter among the 3 prepared pans.

5 Bake for 12 to 14 minutes, or until a cake tester or wooden toothpick inserted in the center comes out clean. Allow the layers to cool completely in the pans. Run the tip of a blunt knife around the edge of each pan to release the cake. Turn out onto cooling racks and carefully peel off the paper liners.

black-and-white park avenue cake

A checkerboard cake is nothing new, but the effect is quite dramatic. To make this cake, you will need a checkerboard cake pan set with pans 8 to 9 inches in diameter. These sets, which come in threes, are available in cookware shops, craft stores, and by mail order (see page 214).

3 cups cake flour

2 cups sugar

4 1/2 teaspoons baking powder

1/2 teaspoon salt

2 sticks (8 ounces) unsalted butter, at room temperature

1 1/4 cups buttermilk

4 whole eggs

2 egg yolks

2 teaspoons vanilla extract

2 ounces unsweetened chocolate, melted and cooled

2 ounces white chocolate, melted and cooled

Semisweet Ganache (page 165)

White Chocolate Buttercream (page 83)

Dark chocolate candy wafers or chocolate chunks, for decoration

MAKES AN 8 1/2-INCH TRIPLE-LAYER CAKE: SERVES 12 TO 16

1 Preheat the oven to 350 degrees F. Butter three checkerboard cake pans, 8 to 9 inches in diameter. Line the bottoms with parchment or waxed paper and butter the paper.

2 Place the flour, sugar, baking powder, and salt in a large mixer bowl. With the mixer on low speed, blend for 30 seconds. Add the butter and 1 cup of the buttermilk and beat just until combined and evenly moistened. Raise the speed to medium and beat until light and fluffy, 2 to 3 minutes.

3 In a medium bowl, whisk together the whole eggs, egg yolks, remaining 1/4 cup buttermilk, and vanilla. Add to the batter in 2 or 3 additions, scraping down the sides of the bowl well and beating only until incorporated after each addition; do not overmix.

4 To make the dark chocolate batter, whisk 1 cup of the vanilla batter into the melted unsweetened chocolate, then gently whisk in another 3 cups batter.

5 For the white batter, whisk 1 cup of the vanilla batter into the melted white chocolate and whisk back into the remaining vanilla batter in the bowl as gently as possible. Using the dividers provided in the set and two 14-inch pastry bags fitted with plain 3/8-inch tips, fill the pans about half full. The cakes will rise to the top when done. You'll need 2 layers with 2 chocolate rings each and 1 layer with 2 vanilla rings.

CONTINUED

163 cakes with a world of flavor

6 Bake for about 25 minutes, or until a cake tester or wooden toothpick inserted in the center comes out clean. Allow the layers to cool in the pans for 10 minutes. Turn out onto wire racks. Peel off the paper and let cool completely.

7 To assemble the cake, place one of the layers with 2 chocolate rings on a cake stand or large serving plate. Spoon half of the Semisweet Ganache onto the cake and spread it evenly over the layer, leaving a generous $^{1}/_{4}$-inch margin around the edges. Place the only layer with 2 vanilla rings onto the cake. Spread a similar amount of ganache over this layer, again leaving a $^{1}/_{4}$-inch margin. Top with the final cake layer, aligning the sides carefully so that the pattern will be successful. To make frosting easier, you may want to refrigerate the cake briefly to allow the ganache to set up first. This will ensure that the squares line up smartly.

8 Frost the sides and top with the White Chocolate Butter-cream, carefully smoothing out the frosting. Decorate the cake with chocolate candy wafers or chocolate chunks.

6 ounces semisweet chocolate, coarsely chopped

$^{1}/_{2}$ cup heavy cream

semisweet ganache MAKES ABOUT 1 CUP

Place the chocolate in a heatproof bowl. Heat the cream to a simmer, pour over the chocolate, and let stand for 5 minutes. Whisk until smooth.

black forest cake

Dark chocolate, whipped cream, brandied cherries . . . what's not to like about this confection that originated in Germany's Black Forest, a region renowned for its cherries, and the clear brandy, Kirschwasser, distilled from them? Dark cherries steeped in brandy are an essential ingredient of this world-class dessert. You can buy brandied Morello cherries at specialty food shops and online (see page 212). Purchased are pricey though, so you may decide to make your own as directed on page 168. It's easy if you leave them enough time; the cherries and brandy have to keep company for at least several hours and are better after spending the night together.

3/4 cup plus 2 tablespoons cake flour

3/4 cup unsweetened cocoa powder

7 eggs

1 3/4 cups sugar

3 cups heavy cream

1 1/2 teaspoons vanilla extract

Brandied Cherries (page 168), well drained, brandy reserved

Chilled chocolate curls, for decoration (see page 21)

MAKES A 9-INCH TRIPLE-LAYER CAKE; SERVES 16 TO 20

1 Preheat the oven to 350 degrees F. Line the bottoms of three 9-inch round cake pans with rounds of parchment or waxed paper but do not grease the pans.

2 Sift together the cake flour and cocoa powder. Set these dry ingredients aside.

3 With an electric mixer in a large mixer bowl, beat the eggs to blend. Gradually add 1 1/2 cups of the sugar and beat on medium-high speed until a slowly dissolving ribbon forms when the beaters are lifted.

4 Sift a third of the dry ingredients over the egg mixture. With a rubber spatula, gently fold in. Repeat this step twice more, then fold the batter until the ingredients are well mixed without deflating the batter. Divide the batter among the 3 prepared pans.

5 Bake the layers for about 20 minutes, or until a cake tester or wooden toothpick stuck into the center comes out clean. Remove from the oven and let the layers cool in their pans completely, at least 1 hour. To unmold, run a blunt knife around the edges of the pan and invert; peel off the paper.

CONTINUED

6 In a large chilled bowl with chilled beaters, beat the cream until it mounds lightly. Add the remaining ¹/₄ cup sugar and the vanilla and whip until the cream is fairly stiff.

7 To assemble the cake, place a layer, flat side up, on a cake stand or serving plate and sprinkle 2 to 3 tablespoons of the reserved cherry brandy evenly over the top to moisten. Cover the cake with ²/₃ cup of the whipped cream, spreading it all the way to the edge. Arrange half of the cherries on top of the cream. Cover the cherries with another ²/₃ cup whipped cream. Repeat with the second layer. Put the third cake layer on top and moisten it with the remaining cherry brandy. Frost the entire cake—top and sides—with the remaining whipped cream.

8 To decorate, gently scoop up the chilled chocolate curls with your hands and press them into the sides of the cake, covering them completely with curls. Decorate the top, if desired, with rosettes of whipped cream and some extra cherries. Refrigerate the cake for several hours before serving. This will make cutting and serving the cake much easier.

1 pound dark, sweet cherries (see Baker's Note)

¹/₂ cup kirsch

BAKER'S NOTE

If using fresh cherries, halve and pit them and combine them and any juices with the kirsch. If using frozen cherries, first thaw them, then combine them and their juice with the kirsch. If using canned cherries, which should be your last choice, drain the cherries well, reserving ¹/₄ cup of the syrup to combine with the kirsch and drained cherries.

brandied cherries   MAKES ABOUT 2 CUPS

Put the cherries and kirsch into a container with a cover. Refrigerate for several hours or up to several days. For use, drain the cherries well, reserving the liquor in which they steeped.

santa fe blue cornmeal cake with caramel cream

This Southwest-inspired dessert includes ingredients that don't usually show up in cake recipes: blue cornmeal, ground chile, and *cajeta,* which is a thick, dark syrup made from caramelized goat's milk. *Cajeta* is very popular in Mexico. The caramel has an addictive sweet flavor with no trace of goat. The hit of chile may surprise you, but as good cooks have known for a long time, there is lovely synergy between sweet and hot.

³/₄ cup pecan halves

1 ³/₄ cups cake flour

²/₃ cup blue cornmeal
(see Baker's Note, page 171)

2 teaspoons baking powder

2 teaspoons ground cinnamon

1 teaspoon ground chile arbol,
or ¹/₂ teaspoon cayenne pepper
(see Baker's Note, page 171)

1 teaspoon salt

1 ¹/₂ cups sugar

8 eggs, separated

1 ¹/₂ cups buttermilk

4 tablespoons unsalted butter,
melted and cooled slightly

³/₄ cup *cajeta,* warmed until spreadable
(see Baker's Note, page 171)

Caramel Cream (page 171)

MAKES AN 8-INCH TRIPLE-LAYER CAKE; SERVES 12 TO 16

1 Preheat the oven to 350 degrees F. Butter three 8-inch round cake pans. Line the bottom of each pan with a round of parchment or waxed paper and butter the paper. Chop ¹/₂ cup of the pecans and set aside for decoration.

2 In a food processor, combine the flour, cornmeal, baking powder, cinnamon, ground chile, salt, the remaining ¹/₄ cup pecans, and 1 ¹/₄ cups of the sugar. Process just until the pecans are finely chopped. Dump this into a large mixing bowl and make a well in the center. Pour the egg yolks, buttermilk, and melted butter into the well and whisk to combine them all, mixing until smooth.

3 In a large clean mixer bowl, whip the egg whites with the remaining ¹/₄ cup sugar until soft peaks form. Fold about a fourth of the whites into the batter to lighten it. Then gently fold in the remaining whites just until no streaks remain. Divide the batter among the 3 prepared pans.

4 Bake for 21 to 25 minutes, or until a cake tester or wooden toothpick stuck into the center of the cake comes out clean and the cake is beginning to pull away from the sides of the pan. Cool the cakes in their pans on wire racks for 10 minutes, then turn out onto the racks, peel off the paper liners, and let cool completely, at least 1 hour.

CONTINUED

If blue cornmeal is not available, yellow can be used with equally fine results.

O Despite the amount of chile in this cake, the effect is subtle and extremely pleasing. To understand why only half as much cayenne is suggested as a substitute for the first-choice chile arbol, here are a few of the heat ratings in Scoville units for a number of popular chiles: ancho and poblano (1,250 to 2,000), arbol and guajillo (2,000 to 4,500), cayenne (20,000 to 40,000), and habanero (100,000 to 325,000).

O *Cajeta* is usually imported from Mexico and can be found in shops in Latino neighborhoods and in the ethnic foods sections of many supermarkets.

$^1/_2$ cup *cajeta*

3 cups heavy cream

3 tablespoons sugar

5 To assemble the cake, place a layer, flat side up, on a cake stand or serving plate. Dollop $^1/_4$ cup of the *cajeta* over the cake and spread evenly, leaving a $^1/_4$-inch margin around the edges. Top with about $^3/_4$ cup of the Caramel Cream and smooth out with a rubber spatula, spreading it evenly right to the edge of the cake. Repeat these steps with the second layer and another $^1/_4$ cup *cajeta* and $^3/_4$ cup Caramel Cream. Set the top layer in place and spread the remaining $^1/_4$ cup *cajeta* all the way to the edge. Then frost the top of the cake with the remaining Caramel Cream. Decorate with the reserved chopped pecans.

caramel cream   MAKES 4 $^1/_2$ CUPS

1 Put the *cajeta* and $^1/_2$ cup of the heavy cream in a large heatproof bowl and set the bowl over a pan of warm water. Stir just until the *cajeta* dissolves.

2 Remove from the heat and add the sugar and remaining 2 $^1/_2$ cups cream. Beat with an electric mixer until almost stiff.

holiday and special-occasion cakes

chocolate valentine sweetheart cake

Unlike all the other recipes in this book, this ethereal cake contains no flour, which means it lacks the structure to stand as tall as a triple-layered cake usually does. In fact, the entire dessert is less than 3 inches high. What it lacks in height, however, it more than makes up for in richness and flavor.

A seductively spiced ganache, flavored with saffron and cinnamon and subtly spiked with chile, offers a pleasing contrast to the all-chocolate layers. The effect is hard to imagine until you taste it. Let's just say, it could be considered a love potion. The cake layers can be made a day in advance. The frosted cake must be chilled until set, but the dessert should be served at room temperature to fully appreciate both the texture and flavor.

As always, but especially in this intense recipe, you must use absolutely the best bittersweet chocolate you can find. A cocoa content of 65 percent is ideal. With a total of 2 pounds of chocolate in the cake and ganache frosting, this dessert should definitely be offered to those you love, especially those who love chocolate as much as you do.

1 pound bittersweet chocolate

2 sticks (8 ounces) unsalted butter

6 whole eggs

6 egg yolks

²/₃ cup packed light brown sugar

²/₃ cup unsweetened coconut milk

Spiced Chocolate Ganache with Coconut Milk and Rosewater (page 177)

1 small rose or a small spray of rosebuds, for decoration

MAKES A HEART-SHAPED TRIPLE-LAYER CAKE; SERVES 12 TO 16

1 Preheat the oven to 300 degrees F. Butter 3 heart-shaped 7 ¹/₂-inch pans, about 1 ¹/₂ inches high. Line the bottoms with parchment or waxed paper and butter the paper.

2 With a large sharp chef's knife, coarsely chop the chocolate. Divide the butter into tablespoons. Place the chocolate and butter in a large heatproof bowl and set over barely simmering water. Cook, stirring, until melted, 10 to 15 minutes. Remove from the heat and whisk in the eggs, egg yolks, brown sugar, and coconut milk, taking care not to whip in an excess amount of air. Divide the batter among the 3 prepared pans.

CONTINUED

3 Bake for 20 to 25 minutes, or until the layers are set only around the edges and still retain an area about 3 inches in diameter in the center that remains shimmery, loose, and shiny; this part will set up when the cake cools. Do not let the layers bake so long that the batter rises over the tops of the pans; over baking will cause the cake to rise up and then sink back down like a soufflé, and the texture will suffer for it. Let the layers cool to room temperature. Cover the cakes in the pans and refrigerate for at least several hours, or overnight, until firmly set.

4 To remove the cakes from the pans, carefully and gently warm the bottom of one layer on the stove top over low heat for just a few moments. Invert onto a cake plate or platter and tap out the layer. Peel off the paper. Repeat with the remaining layers.

5 To assemble the cake, spread about $1/4$ cup of the Spiced Chocolate Ganache over the first layer. Place the next layer on top and repeat. Place the third layer on top and pour $3/4$ cup ganache onto the cake, spreading to coat the top and sides. Decorate with a small rose or a spray of rosebuds.

1 pound bittersweet chocolate

²/₃ cup unsweetened coconut milk

²/₃ cup heavy cream

3 cinnamon sticks, broken up

1 small dried hot red pepper

1 teaspoon loosely packed saffron threads

¹/₂ vanilla bean, split lengthwise

1 tablespoon rosewater

spiced chocolate ganache with coconut milk and rosewater MAKES ABOUT 2 ¹/₂ CUPS

Many years ago, an article in Saveur *magazine by Cuban food writer and restaurateur Maricel Presilla, author of* The New Taste of Chocolate, *detailed a spiced hot chocolate drink called* agasajos, *traditionally served in Spain at receptions during the seventeenth century. The intriguing blend of spices and chocolate is used here to produce a heavenly ganache unlike any you have ever tasted.*

1 With a large chef's knife, coarsely chop the chocolate and place it in a heatproof bowl.

2 In a medium nonreactive saucepan, combine the coconut milk, cream, cinnamon sticks, hot pepper, and saffron. With the tip of a small knife, scrape the tiny seeds from the vanilla bean into the cream; add the pod, too. Bring to a simmer and continue to cook over the lowest heat for 10 minutes. Remove from the heat.

3 Discard the hot pepper at once. Allow the cream to infuse for 10 minutes longer. Strain the warm cream over the chopped chocolate and add the rosewater. Let stand for about 10 minutes, then whisk until smooth.

halloween sweet potato cake

Pale orange cake moist with sweet potato, covered with a light, creamy chocolate frosting, offers the perfect dessert for an autumn holiday like Halloween. While you could bake the sweet potato in advance, the batter comes together more easily when the potato puree is warm.

Decorate the frosted cake, if you like, with candy corn or small candy pumpkins. (A deft change of decoration could easily transform this into a Thanksgiving cake.)

2 medium or 1 large sweet potato
(about 12 ounces)

3 cups cake flour

3 teaspoons baking powder

1 1/2 teaspoons ground cinnamon

3/4 teaspoon grated nutmeg

1/4 teaspoon ground cloves

5 eggs, separated

2 1/4 cups sugar

1 stick plus 2 tablespoons (5 ounces)
unsalted butter, at room temperature

1 1/2 teaspoons vanilla extract

1 1/4 cups milk

Chocolate Cream Cheese Frosting
(page 181)

Orange Cream Filling (page 181)

MAKES A 9-INCH TRIPLE-LAYER CAKE; SERVES 16 TO 20

1 Preheat the oven to 400 degrees F. Prick the sweet potatoes in 2 or 3 places, set in a small baking dish, and bake for 1 hour, or until the potatoes are very soft and their juices are oozing. Remove from the oven and let cool slightly.

2 Reduce the oven temperature to 350 degrees F. Butter the bottoms and sides of three 9-inch round cake pans. Line with rounds of parchment or waxed paper and butter the paper.

3 As soon as the sweet potatoes are cool enough to handle, peel off the skin and remove any dark spots. Cut the potatoes into chunks and put into a food processor. Puree until smooth. Measure out 1 cup sweet potato puree for this recipe. Any leftover is cook's bonus.

4 Sift together the flour, baking powder, cinnamon, nutmeg, and ground cloves. Set these dry ingredients aside.

5 In a large mixer bowl with an electric mixer on medium speed, beat the egg whites until frothy. Raise the speed to high and gradually beat in 1/4 cup of the sugar. Continue to beat until the egg whites form moderately stiff peaks.

CONTINUED

6 In another large bowl, combine the sweet potato puree, softened butter, vanilla, and the remaining 2 cups sugar. Beat until the mixture is light and fluffy. Add the egg yolks one at a time, beating well and scraping down the sides of the bowl after each addition. With the mixer on low speed, add the dry ingredients and milk alternately in 2 or 3 additions, beginning and ending with the dry ingredients. (If using a hand mixer, you'll probably need to use medium-low speed.)

7 With a large rubber spatula, fold in one-fourth of the beaten egg whites to lighten the batter. Then fold in the remainder just until no streaks remain; be sure not to over-mix, or the batter will deflate. Divide the batter among the 3 prepared cake pans.

8 Bake for 25 to 30 minutes, or until a cake tester or wooden toothpick stuck in the center comes out clean and the cake is beginning to pull away from the sides of the pan. Let the layers cool in their pans for 10 minutes. Then turn out onto wire racks, peel off the paper liners, and let cool completely, at least 1 hour.

9 To assemble the cake, put one layer, flat side up, onto a cake stand or serving plate. Fit a pastry bag with a $^1/_2$-inch plain tip and fill with about 1 cup of the Chocolate Cream Cheese Frosting. Pipe a border around the top edge of the cake to create a rim. Fill the center with half the Orange Cream Filling, smoothing it to the chocolate border. Place a second layer on top of the filling, and pipe a border of frosting around it. Fill with the remainder of the filling, again smoothing it to the border. Place the third layer on top of all and use the rest of the frosting to cover the sides and top of the cake.

10 ounces cream cheese,
at room temperature (see Baker's Note)

1 stick (4 ounces) unsalted butter,
at room temperature (see Baker's Note)

1 box (16 ounces)
confectioners' sugar, sifted

1 1/2 ounces unsweetened chocolate,
melted and cooled slightly

BAKER'S NOTE

Remove the butter and cream cheese from
the refrigerator in plenty of time to allow
both to become very soft before you start.

1 cup sweetened cream cheese and
butter mixture, reserved in step 2 of the
Chocolate Cream Cheese Frosting
(recipe above)

2 tablespoons frozen orange juice
concentrate, thawed

1/4 teaspoon orange extract

chocolate cream cheese frosting
MAKES 3 CUPS

1 In a large mixer bowl, beat together the cream cheese
and butter until well blended. Gradually add the confectioners' sugar in batches, sifting or shaking it through a sieve
and scraping down the sides of the bowl several times. Beat
until the mixture is light and fluffy, 2 to 3 minutes.

2 Measure out 1 cup of the sweetened butter and cream
cheese and set aside for the orange cream filling.

3 Beat the melted chocolate into the remainder of
the cream cheese mixture until thoroughly incorporated.
Use at once.

orange cream filling   MAKES ABOUT 1 CUP

Stir together the sweetened cream cheese and butter,
orange juice concentrate, and orange extract until well
blended.

ice cream birthday cake

○○○

In many families, ice cream cake is the birthday dessert of choice, especially because it's so popular with kids. In fact, this recipe was kitchen tested by a thirteen-year-old. The extra-simple version of chocolate cake features a batter mixed in one bowl and containing no eggs at all. That's because a sturdy cake is needed to stand up to the ice cream. Extra sugar in the batter prevents the layers, which are served frozen, from becoming too hard.

This is the only cake in the book that is made up of only two cake layers; the third comes from the thick layer of ice cream. The dessert looks really neat as a square, but if you prefer a round cake, be sure to use a 9-inch pan. To turn the cake into a birthday cake, candles are a must. If you want to write an inscription on top, the easiest way is with purchased tubes of colored frosting.

One-Bowl Chocolate Cake (page 185)

1 half-gallon ice cream, any kind

$\frac{1}{2}$ cup prepared caramel sauce, fudge sauce, or another complementary flavor

$\frac{1}{2}$ cup chopped nuts, coarse cookie crumbs, mini chocolate chips, or small candies, such as M&M's, plus extra for decoration

8 ounces semisweet or bittersweet chocolate

$\frac{1}{2}$ cup heavy cream

2 tablespoons light corn syrup

MAKES A TRIPLE-LAYER 8-INCH DESSERT; SERVES 14 TO 16

1 Bake the cake layers as directed.

2 When the cake layers are cool, prepare the ice cream filling. Allow the ice cream to soften enough to work with, but do not let it melt. Place the ice cream in a large bowl and, with a heavy spoon, stir enough to make it malleable. Pour the sauce over it, sprinkle with the nuts or candy, and fold them in a few times to make ribbons.

3 Line an 8-inch square cake pan with enough plastic wrap to allow a few inches to drape over the sides. Dump the ice cream filling into the lined pan and pack it down evenly to remove any gaps.

CONTINUED

BAKER'S NOTE

If you have trouble slicing the frozen cake, simply dip your knife in a glass of hot water, then wipe it dry, between cuts.

4 While the ice cream is still softened, set one of the cake layers on top, flat side up, and press down gently to remove any gaps. Cover with more plastic wrap and place it in the freezer for at least 2 hours to set well; immediately adjust the freezer to a colder setting so it will help set the cake fast. Place the remaining layer on a large serving plate and cover with plastic until it is needed.

5 When you're ready to finish assembling the dessert, make a chocolate glaze. Place the chocolate in a heatproof bowl, breaking it up first if it is in large pieces. In a small saucepan, heat the cream and corn syrup to a simmer. Pour this hot liquid over the chocolate and let stand for 5 minutes. Whisk until smooth, then let cool for about 2 minutes before using to allow it to set a little.

6 Remove the cake and ice cream from the freezer. Unmold by pulling the excess plastic and inverting the cake and ice cream onto a serving plate. Remove all the plastic. Top with the reserved layer of cake. Pour the chocolate glaze onto the center of the cake and carefully spread it around, allowing it to drizzle over the sides and collect on the plate. Return the dessert to the freezer to set for at least 30 minutes, or up to 2 hours.

7 Before serving, decorate the top edge with additional candies and/or nuts. Let the dessert stand at room temperature for 10 to 15 minutes before slicing, so you can get a knife through it.

1 1/2 cups all-purpose flour

1 1/4 cups sugar

1/4 cup unsweetened cocoa powder

1 teaspoon baking soda

1/2 teaspoon baking powder

1/2 teaspoon salt

1/3 cup neutral vegetable oil, such as soybean, canola, or vegetable blend

1 cup water

1 teaspoon vanilla extract

one-bowl chocolate cake

MAKES 2 SQUARE 8-INCH LAYERS OR 2 ROUND 9-INCH LAYERS

1 Preheat the oven to 350 degrees F. Butter two 8-inch square cake pans. Line the bottoms with parchment or waxed paper; butter the paper.

2 Sift the flour, sugar, cocoa powder, baking soda, baking powder, and salt into a large mixing bowl. Use a wire whisk to blend the dry ingredients thoroughly.

3 Add the oil and 1/2 cup of the water to the dry ingredients and whisk until smooth. Add another 1/2 cup water and the vanilla and again whisk until smooth. Divide the batter between the two prepared cake pans.

4 Bake the cake layers for 18 to 20 minutes, or until a cake tester or wooden toothpick inserted in the center comes out clean. Allow to cool for 10 minutes; then invert onto cooling racks, remove the paper liners, and let cool completely, at least 1 hour.

chocolate-raspberry wedding cake

Chocolate lovers deserve to enjoy their favorite flavor, even on their wedding day. This dark triple-tiered beauty makes no compromises. Layers of moist chocolate butter cake are filled with raspberry preserves, frosted with chocolate ganache spiked with brandy, and decorated with an abundance of fresh raspberries. The square shape gives the cake elegant proportions, a pleasing change from the usual round, and the layers are cut into narrow rectangles for serving.

Note that each tier is a separate triple-layer cake. Because of the size restrictions of a home kitchen—you cannot get 9 baking pans in your oven at the same time—each tier is baked separately. The instructions for mixing, filling, and frosting are the same for each and are given only once, but the proportions of ingredients and baking times change with size.

The cake layers can be baked 3 to 4 days in advance, wrapped well, stacked on a cake board (3 to a board), and stored in the refrigerator. (If you place the layers on a cake board after they are wrapped to support them during storage, the board should still be usable during assembly.) If you have room to refrigerate the finished cake, it can be filled and frosted a day ahead. The advantage is that the cake will travel well without softening too much while it sits at room temperature the next day.

3 triple-layer Chocolate Butter Cakes,
6, 8, and 10 inches in diameter
(pages 189–190)

Bittersweet Brandied Ganache
(page 191)

3 cups seedless raspberry preserves

4 cups fresh raspberries,
any color or combination

MAKES A THREE-TIERED (6-, 8-, AND 10-INCH) SQUARE TRIPLE-LAYER CAKE; SERVES 100 (OR 80 TO 85 IF THE TOP TIER IS RESERVED)

1 Up to 4 days in advance, bake the 3 Chocolate Butter Cakes (9 layers in all) as directed. After they have cooled, wrap the layers well in plastic, set each on an appropriately sized cake board that will support it, and refrigerate.

2 Make the Bittersweet Brandied Ganache shortly before you plan to frost the cake.

CONTINUED

187 holiday and special-occasion cakes

3 To assemble the wedding cake, place one 6-inch layer on the same size cake board; use the same one the cake was stored on. Spread $1/3$ cup of the raspberry preserves evenly over the cake, leaving a $1/4$-inch margin around the edge. Repeat with the second layer and another $1/3$ cup preserves. Set the third layer in place and frost the top and sides with 2 cups of the Bittersweet Brandied Ganache. Use a clean palette knife to create sharp corners and edges; if needed, warm the knife briefly under warm—not hot—water and quickly wipe dry before smoothing. Refrigerate the 6-inch tier, and the two remaining tiers, as they are finished.

4 For the 8-inch tier, spread $1/2$ cup preserves between the layers and frost with 3 cups of the ganache.

5 For the 10-inch tier, use $2/3$ cup preserves and $3 1/4$ cups ganache.

6 With a sharp serrated knife, trim all 8 of the plastic dowels so that they are $1/2$ inch taller than the 3 finished cakes. Be sure to cut straight and evenly. Press 4 of the dowels into the 10-inch cake 4 inches in from the edge to create a 6-inch square pattern in the center. Repeat with the 4 remaining dowels, setting them into the 8-inch tier to form a 4-inch square in the center.

7 Set the cake stand on the table. Using a carpenter's level, make sure the stand is level; shim with small strips of cardboard, if necessary. Carefully stack the cakes on their boards in the center of the stand. Using a pastry bag fitted with a $3/8$-inch plain tip and filled with the remaining ganache, camouflage the cake boards by piping dots of frosting in a single row around the joined edges. Refrigerate the cake for at least 4 hours and preferably overnight. Transport, if necessary, cold, and let return to room temperature before serving.

8 To finish decorating, set a silver sugar bowl or small vase in the center of the top tier and fill with berries. Or simply pile up raspberries on top of the cake, letting the berries cascade down the sides and around the base of the cake.

9 To serve, cut the cake into rectangular pieces about 2 inches long and 1 inch wide. The tiers should yield 18, 32, and 50 slices, respectively.

6-inch chocolate butter cake   MAKES 3 LAYERS

2 cups cake flour

2 cups sugar

1 cup unsweetened cocoa powder, *not* Dutch process

2 1/2 teaspoons baking soda

1/2 teaspoon ground cinnamon

1/2 teaspoon salt

2 sticks (8 ounces) unsalted butter, at room temperature

1 cup buttermilk

2 eggs

1 cup freshly brewed coffee, cooled to room temperature

1 Preheat the oven to 350 degrees F. Butter three 6-inch square cake pans. Line the bottoms with parchment or waxed paper and butter the paper.

2 In a large mixer bowl, combine the flour, sugar, cocoa, baking soda, cinnamon, and salt. With the electric mixer on low speed, blend for about 30 seconds. Add the butter and buttermilk and blend on low until moistened. Raise the speed to medium and beat until light and fluffy, 2 to 3 minutes.

3 Whisk the eggs and coffee together, and add to the batter in 3 additions, scraping down the sides of the bowl and beating only until blended after each addition. Divide the batter among the 3 prepared pans; each 6-inch pan will take just slightly more than 2 cups.

4 Bake the layers for 35 minutes, or until a cake tester or wooden toothpick inserted in the center comes out clean. Allow the cakes to cool in the pans for about 15 minutes. Carefully turn them out onto wire racks and allow to cool completely. Remove the paper liners only when they are cool.

CONTINUED

3 cups cake flour

3 cups sugar

1 1/2 cups unsweetened cocoa powder,
not Dutch process

3 teaspoons baking soda

3/4 teaspoon ground cinnamon

3/4 teaspoon salt

3 sticks (12 ounces) unsalted butter,
at room temperature

1 1/2 cups buttermilk

3 eggs

1 1/2 cups freshly brewed coffee,
cooled to room temperature

8-inch chocolate butter cake   MAKES 3 LAYERS

Use three 8-inch square cake pans and follow the instructions on page 189 for the 6-inch cake. Each pan will take about 3 1/4 cups of batter. Bake for 38 to 40 minutes, or until a cake tester or wooden toothpick inserted in the center comes out clean.

4 cups cake flour

4 cups sugar

2 cups unsweetened cocoa powder,
not Dutch process

4 teaspoons baking soda

1 teaspoon ground cinnamon

1 teaspoon salt

1 pound unsalted butter,
at room temperature

2 cups buttermilk

4 eggs

2 cups freshly brewed coffee,
cooled to room temperature

10-inch chocolate butter cake   MAKES 3 LAYERS

Use three 10-inch square cake pans and follow the instructions on page 189 for the 6-inch cake. Each pan will take about 4 1/2 cups of batter. Bake for 40 to 45 minutes, or until a cake tester or wooden toothpick inserted in the center comes out clean.

3 1/2 pounds bittersweet chocolate, broken up

3 1/2 sticks (14 ounces) unsalted butter, cut up

3 1/2 cups heavy cream, heated slightly to remove the chill

2/3 cup brandy or Cognac

bittersweet brandied ganache   MAKES ABOUT 10 CUPS

1 Place the chocolate and butter in a large heatproof bowl. Set the bowl over a pot of barely simmering water. As the chocolate and butter melt, stir to blend.

2 When completely melted, remove from the heat and whisk in first the cream and then the brandy. Be sure to scrape down the bowl well and mix thoroughly. Allow to cool and thicken to the consistency of mayonnaise.

lavender-rose wedding cake

**WEDDING CAKE ELEMENTS
AND TIMETABLE**

○ Prepare the Lavender-Rose-Raspberry Jelly at least 4 days and up to a month before the wedding.

○ Make the Lavender-Rose Syrup up to a week in advance.

○ Bake all the Vanilla Buttermilk Cakes at least 2 days in advance. If wrapped well and refrigerated, they can be made up to 5 days ahead.

○ Make the Rose Buttercream Frosting shortly before assembling the cake.

○ Frost the cakes at least 4 hours and preferably a day in advance. If you have room in the refrigerator, the wedding cake can be completely finished a day in advance.

○ Assemble the cake on the table on which it will be presented no more than 4 hours in advance.

3 triple-layer Vanilla Buttermilk Cakes, 6, 9, and 12 inches in diameter (pages 196–198)

Lavender-Rose Syrup (page 196)

Lavender-Rose-Raspberry Jelly (page 195)

Rose Buttercream Frosting (page 199)

Truly glorious and elegant in its simplicity, this floral cake exhibits extremely good taste while it steals the show. Cleanly frosted with ivory buttercream, it has no fondant and no froufrou piping. An abundance of roses adorns the cake, along with a few sprigs of lavender.

True, the instructions are lengthy, and you do need special equipment, but so much more goes into a wedding cake. Because each element—the cakes, filling, and frosting—is made in advance, if you can carve out enough refrigerator space to chill first the nine layers and then the finished cake, the assembly will not be stressful. Because of the volume of batter mixed and baked to produce a cake this large, this recipe is actually composed of three cakes. It's the only way to accomplish so much in a home kitchen.

Having prepared all the elements for the cake, here's how to put them together to make the most beautiful wedding cake you've ever seen.

MAKES A THREE-TIERED (6-, 9-, AND 12-INCH) ROUND TRIPLE-LAYER CAKE; SERVES ABOUT 120 (OR 86 IF THE TOP TIER IS RESERVED)

1 Bake the 3 Vanilla Buttermilk Cakes (9 layers in all) as directed. If any of the layers has a mounded top, trim it level with a long serrated knife. Place a layer, bottom side up, on the same-size cardboard cake board. All 3 tiers (3 layers each) are filled and frosted the same way; only the amounts change. You should have more than enough for all 3 cakes.

2 Brush each bottom layer lightly with Lavender-Rose Syrup to moisten, then cover it with a thin layer of Lavender-Rose-Raspberry Jelly, leaving a margin of ¹/₄ inch around the edges. Take care not to apply the jelly too thickly or the layers may slide apart. Place the second layer of each size cake on top of the first. Brush lightly with syrup and cover thinly with jelly, again leaving a ¹/₄-inch margin. Put the top layers in place and brush each lightly with syrup only.

CONTINUED

- A decorator's turntable

- A carpenter's level

- Nine $3/4$-inch hollow plastic
  dowel rods

- 1 (12-inch) cake board

- 1 (9-inch) cake board

- 1 (6-inch) cake board

- A silver platter, cake stand, or cake
  plateau at least 16 inches in diameter

- At least 4 dozen perfect tea roses or
  other small roses, partially open,
  greenery attached (one color or
  several—your choice)

- A few sprigs of fresh or dried lavender

3 Apply a crumb coat using 3 to 4 cups of the frosting in all;
cover all 3 cakes with a very thin layer of Rose Buttercream
Frosting to seal in the crumbs and give the cake a more
professional appearance. (A decorator's turntable is essential for this step; for instructions, see page 20.) Once the
crumb coat is in place, refrigerate the cake until the frosting
is set and hard, at least 45 to 60 minutes. Set the remaining
buttercream aside at room temperature.

4 To frost the cakes, remove the 3 cakes from the refrigerator one at a time and apply the finishing layer of frosting
while they are cold. (For general frosting directions, see page
19.) For the 12-inch cake, use 4 $1/2$ to 5 cups of frosting; for
the 9-inch cake, use about 3 cups; and for the 6-inch cake,
use about 1 $1/2$ cups. Smooth out the frosting on the top and
sides to make a neat, sharp edge. While holding a palette
knife or offset spatula in one hand, turn the wheel with the
other and simultaneously lift and lower the knife repeatedly
from the top to the bottom of the cake all around to create
a zigzag pattern and eliminate any bubbles or rough spots
in the frosting. To decorate the top, place the palette knife in
the center and gently drag it out to the edge and pull it back
in a curved motion, simultaneously turning the wheel and
repeating all the way around to form a large daisylike pattern. Refrigerate the frosted cakes for at least several hours,
or preferably overnight.

5 Assemble the wedding cake by placing a platter or cake
plateau at least 16 inches in diameter on the table on which
the cake will be presented. Use a carpenter's level to be sure
it is absolutely flat and level; shim with small pieces of cardboard, if necessary. Place the 12-inch cake on the cake stand.
With a sharp serrated knife, trim 9 hollow plastic dowels so
that they are 5 $1/2$ inches long. Be sure to trim them level;
all must be exactly the same size. Insert the dowels into the
cake tiers as follows before stacking them: With the tip of a
knife, trace a 7-inch circle on top of the 12-inch cake so that
one edge of the circle is flush with what will be the back

edge of the cake. You want wider platforms in front to allow room for the flowers. Press 5 of the dowels evenly spaced around the circle, pushing them all the way through the cake to the cake board. Next trace a 5-inch circle in the back of the 9-inch cake and plant 4 dowels evenly spaced around that circle. Now, carefully stack the 2 tiers. Set the 6-inch tier on top.

6 Build a mound of rose blossoms and floral greens on top of the cake. Fill in gaps between the layers with additional roses and greenery. As a final flourish, drop rose petals around the base of the cake where it meets the table or stand both to decorate and camouflage the cake board at the bottom.

7 To cut the cake, first separate the layers. Remove the plastic dowels. Cut the top cake into 12 to 16 thin wedge-shaped slices. To cut the middle tier, with the tip of your knife, trace one circle about 2 inches in from the edge. Cut the outer ring of cake into about 28 slices 1 inch wide. Cut the inner round into 12 to 16 thin wedges. Draw 2 concentric circles on the largest tier, one 2 inches in from the edge and the second 4 inches in toward the center. Cut the outer ring into 36 one-inch pieces. Cut the middle ring into 24 pieces, and cut the center into 8 slices.

2 ¹/₂ pounds frozen unsweetened raspberries, thawed, juices reserved

1 tablespoon dried lavender

¹/₂ vanilla bean, split lengthwise

1 star anise pod (the whole star)

3 ¹/₂ cups sugar

1 box (1 ³/₄ ounces) pectin

2 tablespoons rosewater

lavender-rose-raspberry jelly   MAKES ABOUT 2 PINTS

This should be prepared at least 4 days and up to one month in advance.

1 Combine the raspberries, lavender, vanilla, and star anise in a large nonreactive saucepan and bring to a boil. Reduce the heat to low and simmer for 20 minutes. In 2 or 3 batches, pour the berry mixture into a mesh strainer set over a bowl to catch the juices. Press to extract as much liquid as possible. This should yield about 2 ¹/₂ cups juice.

CONTINUED

2 Return the juice to the saucepan and add the sugar; stir to dissolve the sugar. Bring to a rolling boil and add the pectin and rosewater. Stir to dissolve the pectin and continue to boil for 1 full minute.

3 Remove from the heat and pour into two clean, hot 1-pint jars. Set the lids in place and screw the bands on loosely. When the jelly cools, tighten the bands. Store in the refrigerator for at least 4 days and up to 1 month before using.

1 1/2 cups sugar

3 cups water

1 1/2 tablespoons dried lavender blossoms

3 tablespoons rosewater

lavender-rose syrup   MAKES 3 CUPS

Combine the sugar, water, and lavender in a small heavy saucepan. Bring to a boil and continue to cook until the syrup is reduced to 3 cups. Strain to remove the lavender. Stir in the rosewater and let cool completely before using.

6 2/3 cups cake flour

4 1/3 cups sugar

3 tablespoons baking powder

1 teaspoon salt

1 pound plus 3 tablespoons unsalted butter, at room temperature

2 3/4 cups buttermilk

9 whole eggs

4 egg yolks

1 1/2 tablespoons vanilla extract

12-inch vanilla buttermilk cake   MAKES 3 LAYERS

Most conventional ovens will not accommodate three 12-inch pans, and you may need to bake this cake in 2 batches. See step 4.

1 Preheat the oven to 325 degrees F. Butter three 12-inch round cake pans. Line the bottom of each pan with a round of parchment or waxed paper and butter the paper.

2 Combine the cake flour, sugar, baking powder, and salt in a large mixer bowl. With the mixer on low speed, blend for 30 seconds. Add the butter and 2 cups of the buttermilk. Mix on low speed briefly to blend; then raise the speed to medium and beat until light and fluffy, 2 to 3 minutes. Because this is such a large amount of batter, at this point, you will need to finish the cake by hand.

3 Pour the batter into a very large (10- to 12-quart) shallow bowl. In a smaller bowl, whisk together the whole eggs, egg yolks, vanilla, and the remaining 3/4 cup buttermilk until well blended. Pour one-third of the egg mixture into the cake batter and fold in completely with a large rubber or silicone spatula. Repeat this step twice with the remaining egg mixture, folding it in completely after each addition. There will be about 15 3/4 cups of batter. Measure out 5 1/4 cups for each of the 3 prepared pans.

4 Bake for about 35 minutes, or until a cake tester or wooden toothpick inserted in the center comes out clean. Note: Most ovens will accommodate only 2 pans of this size. If that is the case, cover and refrigerate the remaining batter immediately. When the other cakes come out, pour the batter into its prepared pan and bake separately. Allow the cakes to cool in their pans for 15 minutes.

5 Turn the layers out onto wire racks by placing a rack on top of a pan, inverting it, and lifting off the pan. Peel off the paper liners and let cool completely. When the layers have cooled, place a cardboard cake board on top of a layer, invert again, and lift off the rack. To make the layers easier to handle, wrap them on their boards completely in plastic, so they don't dry out, and refrigerate them.

CONTINUED

3 3/4 cups cake flour

2 1/2 cups sugar

1 tablespoon plus 2 3/4 teaspoons
baking powder

1/2 teaspoon salt

2 1/2 sticks (10 ounces) unsalted butter,
at room temperature

1 1/4 cups plus 1/3 cup buttermilk

5 whole eggs

2 egg yolks

2 1/2 teaspoons vanilla extract

9-inch vanilla buttermilk cake   MAKES 3 LAYERS

Prepare the cake using the detailed instructions for the 12-inch cake, but use three 9-inch round cake pans. In step 3, there's no need to transfer the batter to a separate bowl. Instead, complete the batter in the mixer bowl, adding the eggs in 2 or 3 additions and beating just until blended. There will be 9 cups of batter; pour 3 cups batter into each pan. Bake for 26 to 28 minutes, or until a cake tester or wooden toothpick inserted in the center comes out clean. After the layers have cooled completely, wrap them in plastic and refrigerate.

1 1/2 cups cake flour

1 cup sugar

2 1/4 teaspoons baking powder

1/4 teaspoon salt

1 stick (4 ounces) unsalted butter,
at room temperature

2/3 cup buttermilk

2 whole eggs

1 egg yolk

1 teaspoon vanilla extract

6-inch vanilla buttermilk cake   MAKES 3 LAYERS

Prepare the cake as instructed in the preceding recipe but use three 6-inch round cake pans. There will be 3 1/3 cups batter; pour slightly more than 1 cup into each pan. Bake for 22 to 24 minutes, or until a cake tester or a wooden tooth-pick inserted in the center comes out clean. After the layers have cooled completely, wrap them in plastic and refrigerate.

10 egg whites

3 1/2 cups sugar

3/4 cup water

2 1/2 pounds unsalted butter,
at room temperature

2 tablespoons vanilla extract

2 tablespoons rosewater

rose buttercream frosting   MAKES ABOUT 12 CUPS

1 Put the egg whites in a large mixer bowl and set up the mixer for use. In a medium heavy saucepan, combine the sugar and water. Warm over medium heat, stirring to dissolve the sugar. Bring to a boil and cook, without stirring, washing any sugar crystals from the sides of the pan with a wet pastry brush, until the syrup reaches the soft-ball stage, 238 degrees F on a candy thermometer. Remove from the heat.

2 Beat the egg whites on medium-low speed until frothy. While beating, gradually pour in the hot sugar syrup in a thin stream, taking care not to hit the beaters. Continue to whip until the mixture is lukewarm and a stiff meringue has formed.

3 Reduce the speed to low and add the butter 2 to 3 table-spoons at a time. When all of the butter is incorporated, return the mixer to medium and whip until the buttercream appears to curdle and then suddenly comes together. Add the vanilla and rosewater, and beat until blended.

tiramisu wedding cake

WEDDING CAKE TIMETABLE

- Make the chocolate shavings up to a week in advance. Store them in a covered plastic container in the refrigerator.

- Make the syrup up to 5 days in advance. Keep refrigerated in a covered jar.

- Bake the cake layers 2 days in advance.

- Make the Zabaglione Cream just before you assemble the cake.

- Assemble the cake 6 to 8 hours in advance the day it is to be served. It needs the resting time for the syrup to permeate the cake and for all the flavors to meld.

3 triple-layer Genoise Cakes, 6, 8, and 10 inches in diameter (pages 202–203)

Espresso-Rum Syrup (page 203)

Zabaglione Cream (page 204)

Unsweetened cocoa powder in a shaker, for dusting the cake

4 $^1/_2$ cups chocolate shavings (see page 21)

A classic genoise is cloaked with marsala-flavored cream custard, moistened with Espresso-Rum Syrup, and showered with a blizzard of chocolate shavings to create an original wedding cake that offers all the best of this most popular Italian dessert. Unlike the other two wedding cakes in this book, these tiers are not stacked, which makes assembly much quicker and easier. Instead, the separate cakes are decoratively displayed on separate cake stands of varying heights. You could also suspend them in an S-bend stand, for a floating effect. A stand like this can either be purchased or rented (see the sources on page 214).

MAKES 3 TRIPLE-LAYER CAKES, 6, 8, AND 10 INCHES IN DIAMETER; SERVES ABOUT 80

1 Bake the 3 Genoise Cakes (9 layers in all) as directed. If any of the layers are domed, trim to level with a long, serrated knife. Set a 10-inch layer on a cake board of the same size. Moisten with 6 to 7 tablespoons of the Espresso-Rum Syrup. Top with 2 cups of the Zabaglione Cream, spreading it all the way to the edges. Dust lightly with cocoa powder. Place the second layer on top and repeat. Set the third layer on top, moisten as before, and cover with the cream, but this time shower with chocolate shavings before dusting with cocoa.

2 For the 8-inch cake, repeat the instructions above, using about $^1/_4$ cup syrup and 1 cup Zabaglione Cream for each layer.

3 For the 6-inch cake, repeat the instructions from step 1, using about 2 $^1/_2$ tablespoons syrup and $^1/_2$ cup Zabaglione Cream per layer.

4 Wrap a long foil strip 3 $^1/_2$ inches wide around each completed cake, fastening it securely with tape. Wrap a 4- to 4 $^1/_2$-inch-wide decorative ribbon around the foil on

CONTINUED

each cake, fastening it neatly with double-sided tape underneath, so the tape is invisible. The ribbon will reach to the top of the cake and may extend beyond the edge; this helps keep the chocolate shavings in place.

5 For final assembly, simply set the cakes on cake stands or in their respective holders on an S-bend stand. Since the cream is perishable, refrigerate any leftovers and do not keep for more than 2 days.

6 To cut the cakes, remove the ribbons and foil. Using a sharp serrated knife, cut the 6-inch cake into 12 slices. To cut the 8-inch cake, with the tip of the knife trace a circle 2 inches in from the edge of the cake. Cut the outer ring into about 24 one-inch slices. Then cut the center into 8 slices. To cut the 10-inch cake, trace a circle 2 inches in from the edge. Cut this outer ring into 26 to 28 one-inch pieces. Cut the center of the cake into 12 slices.

11 eggs

1 $^3/_4$ cups sugar

2 teaspoons vanilla extract

2 $^1/_2$ cups all-purpose flour (see Baker's Note)

10-inch genoise cake   MAKES 3 LAYERS

1 Preheat the oven to 350 degrees F. Line the bottoms of three 10-inch round cake pans with rounds of parchment or waxed paper but do not grease them.

2 Lightly beat the eggs in a large heatproof bowl. Gradually whisk in the sugar and set the bowl over a larger pot of barely simmering water. Whisk constantly until the egg mixture darkens slightly and is warm to the touch, 100 degrees F on an instant-read thermometer.

3 Remove from the heat and whisk in the vanilla. With an electric mixer, beat on medium-high speed until a slowly dissolving ribbon forms when the beaters are lifted, about 6 minutes.

BAKER'S NOTE

All-purpose rather than cake flour is used here because you want the cakes to be sturdy enough to stand up to all the moisture of the syrup and custard and still slice well.

4 Sift about a third of the flour over the top of the batter. Quickly and gently fold it in. Repeat 2 more times with the remaining flour, folding just until no white streaks remain. There will be 15 cups of batter; gently pour 5 cups into each of the 3 prepared pans.

5 Bake the cakes for 21 minutes, or until a cake tester or wooden toothpick inserted in the center comes out clean. Transfer to wire racks and let the layers cool completely in their pans. To unmold, run a blunt knife around the edge to release the cakes. Carefully peel off the paper liners.

7 eggs	
1 cup plus 2 tablespoons sugar	
1 1/2 teaspoons vanilla extract	
1 1/2 cups all-purpose flour	

8-inch genoise cake   MAKES 3 LAYERS

Follow the instructions for the 10-inch cake but use three 8-inch round cake pans. Step 3 will take about 4 1/2 minutes. There will be 10 cups of batter; add 3 1/3 cups to each pan. Bake for 18 minutes, or until a cake tester or wooden toothpick inserted in the center comes out clean.

4 eggs

2/3 cup sugar

1 teaspoon vanilla extract

3/4 cup plus 2 tablespoons all-purpose flour

6-inch genoise cake   MAKES 3 LAYERS

Follow the instructions for the 10-inch cake but use three 6-inch round cake pans. Step 3 will take about 3 minutes. There will be 5 cups of batter; add 1 2/3 cups to each pan. Bake for 16 minutes, or until a cake tester or wooden toothpick inserted in the center comes out clean.

1 2/3 cups freshly brewed espresso

1/2 cup sugar

1/2 cup Myers's dark rum

1/4 cup creme de cacao liqueur, light or dark

espresso-rum syrup   MAKES 2 2/3 CUPS

Pour the hot espresso into a heatproof glass jar. Add the sugar and stir until it dissolves. Let cool, then add the rum and creme de cacao.

CONTINUED

4 cups (1 quart) heavy cream

¹/₃ cup confectioners' sugar

8 egg yolks

¹/₂ cup granulated sugar

1 cup marsala

zabaglione cream   MAKES ABOUT 12 CUPS

1 In a large chilled bowl with chilled beaters, whip the cream with the confectioners' sugar until stiff. Cover and refrigerate.

2 Put the egg yolks in a large stainless steel bowl and beat lightly with a whisk. Gradually whisk in the granulated sugar and marsala. Set the bowl over barely simmering water and whisk continuously until the zabaglione becomes very foamy and thick, 135 to 138 degrees F.

3 Immediately remove from the heat and scrape into a mixer bowl. Beat with the electric mixer fitted with the whip attachment on medium-high speed until the zabaglione cools to room temperature and is very thick.

4 Fold in the whipped cream and use immediately.

strawberry surprise-package cake

Perfect for a birthday, shower, anniversary, or even graduation, this stunning cake can be tinted any color you like, or the cake can be "wrapped" with a colored ribbon and bow. If you're artistic, you can even cover the cake with white fondant, and paint it with food coloring. This recipe illustrates a pink cake with a white bow.

Fondant takes a long time to dry, so be sure to begin making the bow at least 2 days before you plan to assemble the cake. When you remove it from its drying container, handle the bow very carefully, because it will be fragile. Enrobed in fondant, the finished cake keeps well in the refrigerator for up to 5 days.

Note that while this cake looks spectacular covered in a sleek sheet of fondant, you can make an easy facsimile by simply frosting the cake very smoothly and tying it up with grosgrain ribbons and a bow.

Fondant Bow (see box on page 210)

1 ½ pounds individually quick-frozen strawberries, thawed, with their juices (see Baker's Note, page 209)

½ cup sugar

1 cinnamon stick

½ star anise pod

1 one-inch piece of vanilla bean, split lengthwise

Strawberry Butter Cake (page 208)

White Chocolate–Cream Cheese Frosting (page 209)

Confectioners' sugar for dusting

36 ounces pink rolled fondant (see Baker's Note, page 209)

18 ounces white rolled fondant (see Baker's Note, page 209)

Royal Icing (page 209)

MAKES AN 8-INCH SQUARE TRIPLE-LAYER CAKE; SERVES 12 TO 16

1 Make a lovely ribbon bow out of fondant as directed. Let dry thoroughly for at least a day; the bow can be formed up to a week in advance.

2 In 2 batches, put the strawberries and their juices in a blender or food processor and puree until smooth; no need to strain. There will be about 2 ¾ cups. Set aside 1 ¼ cups of the puree for the Strawberry Butter Cake.

3 Make a strawberry coulis to use as filling from the remaining puree. In a heavy nonreactive saucepan, add the sugar, cinnamon stick, and star anise. With the tip of a small knife, scrape the tiny vanilla seeds into the pot; add the pod. Bring to a simmer, stirring to dissolve the sugar. Continue to cook, stirring occasionally, until the mixture has visibly thickened and reduced by about half to ¾ cup. To check for thickness, place about a teaspoon on a chilled plate. Set in the freezer for a minute or two and then run

CONTINUED

your fingertip through the coulis; the track should remain. Remove and discard the cinnamon stick, star anise, and vanilla bean pod. Refrigerate the strawberry coulis in a covered container.

4 Bake the Strawberry Butter Cake as directed and let the layers cool completely. Turn the cooled layers over so that the cakes are top side up. If the layers are at all domed, carefully trim them so that they are level. Use a long, sharp serrated knife for this step. It's important for the square look of this cake that everything be very neat and trim.

5 Because the trimmed surfaces will soak up too much syrup, invert the cake layers onto paper-lined cookie sheets so the trimmed side is down. Spread $1/4$ cup of the strawberry coulis thinly but evenly over each layer right to the edge. Refrigerate the layers for about 1 hour to make handling them easier.

6 To finish assembling the cake, begin by stacking two 8-inch square cake boards. Tape them together, making sure that the corrugated tunnels on one are perpendicular to the tunnels on the other; this crisscrossing provides extra strength. If you have a metal serving plate or tray that can accommodate the cake size, the boards are not absolutely necessary. However, the cake will need to fit in the refrigerator, and paper cake boards make this easier to accomplish.

7 Place one cake layer, coulis facing up, on the cake board. Top with about $2/3$ cup of the White Chocolate–Cream Cheese Frosting and spread it to the edge. Repeat with the next layer. Finally, add the third layer and frost the top and sides of the cake with the remaining frosting. Use an offset spatula to do this neatly, and be sure to make the surface as smooth as possible, with sharp edges and corners. Refrigerate the frosted cake until firm, at least 1 hour.

CONTINUED

8 On a flat work surface dusted with sifted confectioners' sugar, roll out the pink fondant to an 18-inch square less than $1/4$ inch thick. Dust with confectioners' sugar and gently roll loosely around your rolling pin like a piecrust. Lift the sheet up over the cake and unroll the fondant, draping it over the cake to cover. With your hands, gently smooth out the fondant, beginning on the top and pressing it neatly down the sides. Use a small knife or straight pizza wheel to trim the bottom.

9 Roll out the white fondant similarly and cut into 4 ribbons about 1 inch wide and 9 inches long. Lightly dab one side of the strips with Royal Icing and press into the cake to attach like ribbons on a package. Using more icing, glue the bow on top. Allow the entire cake to dry thoroughly before transporting, about 3 hours. (The cake covered with fondant will hold well at room temperature for up to 2 days or in the refrigerator for up to 5 days.)

4 $1/2$ cups cake flour

3 cups sugar

5 $1/4$ teaspoons baking powder

$3/4$ teaspoon salt

3 sticks (12 ounces) unsalted butter, at room temperature

1 $1/4$ cups strawberry puree (reserved in step 2 on page 205)

8 egg whites

$2/3$ cup milk

strawberry butter cake MAKES THREE 8-INCH SQUARE LAYERS

1 Preheat the oven to 350 degrees F. Butter three 8-inch square cake pans. Line with parchment or waxed paper and butter the paper.

2 Put the flour, sugar, baking powder, and salt in a large mixer bowl. With the electric mixer on low speed, blend for 30 seconds. Add the butter and strawberry puree and mix to blend the ingredients. Raise the speed to medium and beat until light and fluffy, 2 to 3 minutes; the batter will resemble strawberry ice cream at this point.

3 In another large bowl, whisk together the egg whites and milk to blend. Add the whites to the batter in 2 or 3 additions, scraping down the sides of the bowl well and mixing only to incorporate after each addition. Divide the batter among the 3 prepared pans.

4 Bake the cakes for 30 to 34 minutes, or until a cake tester or wooden toothpick inserted in the center comes out clean. Allow the layers to cool in the pans for 10 to 15 minutes. Invert and turn out onto wire racks and peel off the paper liners. Let stand until completely cooled before assembling the cake, at least 1 hour.

1 pound cream cheese, chilled (see Baker's Note, below)

6 cups confectioners' sugar, sifted if lumpy

6 ounces white chocolate, melted and cooled

2 teaspoons vanilla extract

white chocolate–cream cheese frosting
MAKES ABOUT 5 CUPS

With an electric mixer, beat the cream cheese with the confectioners' sugar in a large mixer bowl until light and fluffy. Add the melted white chocolate and vanilla and blend in. Do not beat excessively at this point, or the frosting will heat up and become too soft.

1 egg white

1 1/3 cups confectioners' sugar

royal icing   MAKES ABOUT 3/4 CUP

Combine the egg white and sugar in a mixer bowl and, with a mixer on medium-high speed, whip until stiff peaks form.

CONTINUED

BAKER'S NOTES

o It may seem surprising that frozen strawberries are used here, but they are always available, no matter what the season, and the quality is consistent.

o Rolled fondant can be found at superstores and other places that sell cake-decorating equipment.

o For this frosting, the cream cheese should be cold—straight from the refrigerator, not at room temperature—because it will soften with the friction of mixing.

HOW TO MAKE A FONDANT BOW

Because the assembly and drying of the fondant bow can take up to 48 hours, make the bow first. It will keep for weeks. You'll need 18 ounces of fondant and the Royal Icing on page 209 for this project.

1 On a flat work surface dusted with sifted confectioners' sugar, roll out about one-third of the fondant into a rectangle 1/8 inch thick; keep the rest covered so it doesn't dry out. Using a small knife or pizza wheel, cut out about 10 strips 3/4 to 1 inch wide, ranging in length from 5 to 8 inches. Repeat twice for a total of about 30 strips of varying lengths; this gives you a few extra.

2 As each batch of strips is finished, drape them over a broom handle or dowel about 1 inch in diameter. Moisten the ends slightly and pinch them together to form teardrop-shaped loops. Allow the loops to dry for about 24 hours.

3 To hold the bow while it dries, line a flat-bottomed 8-inch bowl or plastic container with a small round of waxed paper. Spoon about 1 tablespoon Royal Icing into the center. Gently slip the fondant loops off the dowel. Using the largest loops first, arrange them pointed ends stuck into the icing and loops facing out, so they are lying flat in a circle like the spokes of a wheel. Now add more icing to the center and a layer of slightly smaller loops, this time standing up the row slightly and filling in any spaces below.

4 Keep adding icing and loops until the bow is the desired fullness. The shortest loops fill out the center. Allow the bow to dry thoroughly.

1.

2.

3.

4.

appendix: sources for ingredients, equipment, and decorating supplies

To help you find what you want faster, the merchants listed here have been divided into three categories: Ingredients for Cakes and Frostings, Kitchen and Baking Equipment, and Cake Decorating Equipment and Supplies. However, the divisions are not definitive: Several of the equipment sellers also offer some ingredients and supplies, for example, and are worth checking out if you can't find what you're looking for elsewhere.

ingredients for cakes and frostings

Arrowhead Mills
The Hain Celestial Group
4600 Sleepytime Drive
Boulder, CO 80301
(630) 595-8919

www.arrowheadmills.com

Items for bakers that are sold online (no mail order) include unbleached white flour, pastry flour, and cornmeal. Arrowhead Mills products, which are organically produced, are available at many supermarkets. The company makes blue cornmeal, but this is available only at select retailers, such as Wild Oats.

Atlantic Spice Company
2 Shore Road
P.O. Box 205
North Truro, MA 02652
(800) 316-7965; fax (508) 487-2550

www.atlanticspice.com

Offerings include spices, spice blends, bulk teas, nuts, seeds, and essential oils. Online and mail-order sales are in wholesale quantities (1 pound minimum on most items); smaller quantities are available at the company's retail store on Cape Cod. A twenty-eight-page catalog can be downloaded in PDF format or obtained by phone or written request.

The Baker's Catalogue
55 Billings Farm Road
White River Junction, VT 05001
(800) 827-6836
customercare@kingarthurflour.com

www.bakerscatalogue.com

The Baker's Catalogue is the retail arm of the King Arthur Flour Company, which has been producing fine flours for more than two centuries. The catalog includes many specialty flours, top-quality extracts, nuts, chocolates, and some equipment. A color-illustrated catalog running fifty-plus pages is available by phone, mail, or online request. The company has a "bricks and mortar" retail store in Vermont and sells many of its flours through supermarkets.

Bob's Red Mill Natural Foods
5209 SE International Way
Milwaukie, OR 97222
(800) 349-2173; fax (503) 653-1339

www.bobsredmill.com

Bob's Red Mill products include flours and meals (including blue cornmeal), nuts, baking aids, and spices that are available at many supermarkets and online. Most items are organically produced.

Charles H. Baldwin & Sons
1 Center Street
P.O. Box 372
West Stockbridge, MA 01266
(413) 232-7785; fax (413) 232-0114
ebm125@bcn.net

www.baldwinextracts.com

A family-owned business, Baldwin has manufactured its highly prized Bourbon vanilla extract since 1888. The firm also offers pure anise, almond, coffee, lemon, orange, peppermint, and spearmint extracts and Bourbon vanilla beans. The family sells its products online, by phone and mail order, and at their old-fashioned general store, which opened its doors in 1912.

Chocosphere
(877) 992-4626

www.chocosphere.com

This is an online-only source of chocolate, cocoa, and gianduja from three dozen makers, including such top-of-the-line firms as Callebaut, Cote d'Or, E. Guittard, Green & Black's, Lindt, Santander, Scharffen Berger, Valrhona, and Venchi.

Cook Flavoring Company
200 Sherwood Road
Paso Robles, CA 93446
(800) 735-0545
cooks@cooksvanilla.com

www.cooksvanilla.com

Cook's manufactures high-quality, all-natural extracts, including vanilla, citrus, berry, almond, and various liquor flavors. Cook's "Cookie Vanilla Extract," which combines extracts from Tahitian and Bourbon vanilla beans, is highly recommended for its flavor and ability to stand up to oven heat.

India Tree Gourmet Spices & Specialties
1421 Elliott Avenue West
Seattle, WA 98199
(800) 369-4848 or (206) 270-0293; fax (206) 282-0587
india@indiatree.com

www.indiatree.com

India Tree's products include edible decorations, colored decorating and sanding sugars, all-natural decorating colors, candied whole violets, candied rose and violet petals, and spices. These are sold through retailers, both online and off. The firm's Web site includes color pictures of its products and a store locator.

La Tourangelle
1145 Harbour Way
South Richmond, CA 94804
(866) 688-6457 or (510) 970-9960; fax (510) 970-9964
contact@latourangelle.com

www.latourangelle.com

La Tourangelle is a domestic producer of high-quality toasted walnut oil, which is usually imported. The firm also offers toasted hazelnut and other specialty oils that are produced overseas.

Scharffen Berger Chocolate Maker
914 Heinz Avenue
Berkeley, CA 94710
(800) 930-4528

www.scharffenberger.com

Despite its German-sounding name, Scharffen Berger is a California-based manufacturer of top-quality cocoa, gianduja, and dark and milk chocolates for baking. Now a subsidiary of Hershey Foods Corporation, its products are available online, at upscale supermarkets, and at other select retailers, including company-owned stores in Berkeley, New York, and San Francisco.

kitchen and baking equipment

BakersTools.com
4917 E. Second Avenue
Spokane Valley, WA 99212
(866) 285-2665
cs@bakerstools.com

www.bakerstools.com

An online source of things every baker needs, including cake-decorating bags and tips, cake pans and rings, cake boards, food coloring, flavorings, fondant and the tools to work it, icing and pastry brushes, sifters, shavers, spatulas, turners, and turntables.

Bridge Kitchenware Corp.
711 Third Avenue
New York, NY 10017
(212) 688-4220; fax (212) 758-5387

www.bridgekitchenware.com

Bridge Kitchenware has been selling French copper cookware since 1946. The company's baking equipment includes stainless steel mixing bowls, aluminum cake pans from 3 to 16 inches in diameter, springform pans from 7 to 11 inches in diameter, and the very-hard-to-find mercurial oven thermometer. The firm offers more than 6,000 items at its retail store in New York and has a forty-four-page catalog that can be downloaded free in PDF format.

Chef's Catalog
5070 Centennial Boulevard
Colorado Springs, CO 80919
(800) 884-2433; fax (800) 967-2433
customerservice@ecare.chefscatalog.com

www.chefscatalog.com

The Chef's Catalog is an online seller of kitchen equipment. Items of interest to bakers include cake pans by Anolon, Chicago Metallic, Kaiser, and NordicWare; Kitchen-Aid standing mixers; handheld mixers by Kitchen-Aid and Cuisinart; Waring and Dualit blenders; and Henckels cutlery. The company also takes orders and catalog request by mail and phone.

Cooking.com
2850 Ocean Park Boulevard, Suite 310
Santa Monica, CA 90405
(800) 663-8810 (phone orders);
(877) 999-2433 (customer service)

www.cooking.com

Cooking.com is an online-only seller of bakeware, kitchen tools, mixers, and blenders from such makers as All-Clad, Anolon, Ateco, Calphalon, Chicago Metallic, Cuisinart, DeLonghi, Emile Henry, Hamilton Beach, Kaiser, Kitchen-Aid, NordicWare, Viking, and Waring.

J.B. Prince Company
36 E. 31st Street, 11th Floor
New York, NY 10016-6821
(800) 473-0577 or (212) 683-3553; fax (212) 683-4488

www.jbprince.com

One-stop source for professional cooking and baking equipment, including molds, gadgets, utensils, mixers, and food processors. The company also sells books and chef's apparel. Merchandise is available online or at the showroom on Manhattan's E. 31st Street. A sixteen-page price list can be downloaded in PDF format.

Sur la Table
Seattle Design Center
5701 Sixth Avenue S., Suite 486
Seattle, WA 98108
(800) 243-0852 or (206) 613-6000; fax (206) 613-6137

www.surlatable.com

Offerings for bakers from Sur la Table include plain and springform cake pans by Chicago Metallic, Kaiser, and NordicWare; copper, stainless steel, and stoneware mixing bowls; cake-decorating equipment by Ateco and Wilton; cake boards; cutlery by Henckels and Wüsthof; silicone oven mitts and pot holders; crystallized flowers; food coloring gels; and edible silver and gold leaf. Items can be ordered online, by phone, or by mail, with print catalogs available by those same means. Sur la Table has "bricks and mortar" stores in many parts of the country and an online store locator.

Williams-Sonoma
3250 Van Ness Avenue
San Francisco, CA 94109
(877) 812-6235; fax (702) 363-2541

www.williams-sonoma.com

Williams-Sonoma offers top-of-the-line cooking utensils and equipment, including baking tools, mixers, and food processors, as well as tableware and a limited number of baking ingredients. Products are offered online, in their mail-order catalog, and at retail stores across the country. (The firm's Web site includes a store locator.) Catalogs may be requested online or by phone.

cake decorating equipment and supplies

Confectionery House
975 Hoosick Road
Troy, NY 12180
(518) 279-4250
info@confectioneryhouse.com

www.confectioneryhouse.com

Good prices and a selection of some 6,000 items mark this firm's offerings, among which are foil-covered and frilly cake boards, cake-decorating supplies and equipment (including Wilton products), cake pans, edible decorations, wedding cake supplies, baker's tools, and books.

New York Cake and Baking Distributors
56 W. 22nd Street
New York, NY 10010
(800) 942-2539 or (212) 675-2253; fax (212) 675-7099

www.nycake.com

Cake baking and decorating supplies and equipment, edible decorations, food colors, flavorings, and Callebaut, Valrhona, and Scharffen Berger baking chocolates and cocoas. The company has an online catalog, but takes orders by phone or fax only. A printed catalog can be requested by phone or fax.

Parrish's Cake Decorating Supplies
225 W. 146th Street
Gardena, CA 90248
(310) 324-2253; fax 324-8277
CustomerService@parrishsmagicline.com

www.parrishsmagicline.com

Parrish's is a fourth-generation, family-owned retailer of baking equipment and baking supplies, including top-quality cake pans, food colors, baker's tools, and decorating bags and tips. Company takes orders and catalog requests by phone, fax, or e-mail.

Sweet Celebrations (formerly Maid of Scandinavia)
P.O. Box 39426
Edina, MN 55439-0426
(800) 328-6722
sweetcel@maidofscandinavia.com

www.sweetc.com

Sweet Celebrations has an extensive selection of high-quality chocolates, gianduja, luster dust and gold leaf, cocoas, chocolate transfer sheets, extracts, cake pans, and decorating equipment. The illustrated catalog typically runs to nearly 150 pages and is available by mail or online request.

Wilton Industries
2240 W. 75th Street
Woodridge, IL 60517
(800) 794-5866 or (630) 963-1818;
fax (888) 824-9520 or (630) 963-7196
info@wilton.com

www.wilton.com

Wilton is a leading manufacturer of cake baking and decorating supplies and offers a huge selection of these items both online and through retail distributors. The firm's Web site features illustrated instructions for many of the techniques and procedures used in cake decorating, including wedding cakes. Wilton also publishes books on cake decorating, including an annual yearbook that offers numerous pictures of highly decorated cakes accompanied by detailed instructions.

index

table of equivalents

liquid/dry measurements

U.S.	METRIC
$1/4$ teaspoon	1.25 milliliters
$1/2$ teaspoon	2.5 milliliters
1 teaspoon	5 milliliters
1 tablespoon (3 teaspoons)	15 milliliters
1 fluid ounce (2 tablespoons)	30 milliliters
$1/4$ cup	60 milliliters
$1/3$ cup	80 milliliters
$1/2$ cup	120 milliliters
1 cup	240 milliliters
1 pint (2 cups)	480 milliliters
1 quart (4 cups; 32 ounces)	960 milliliters
1 gallon (4 quarts)	3.84 liters
1 ounce (by weight)	28 grams
1 pound	448 grams
2.2 pounds	1 kilogram

lengths

U.S.	METRIC
$1/8$ inch	3 millimeters
$1/4$ inch	6 millimeters
$1/2$ inch	12 millimeters
1 inch	2.5 centimeters

oven temperatures

FAHRENHEIT	CELSIUS	GAS
250	120	$1/2$
275	140	1
300	150	2
325	160	3
350	180	4
375	190	5
400	200	6
425	220	7
450	230	8
475	240	9
500	260	10